Reader's Digest Needlecraft Guides

CROCHET & LACEMAKING

Reader's Digest Needlecraft Guides

CROCHET & LACEMAKING

Step-by-step diagrams for every stitch and technique

Published by The Reader's Digest Association Limited
LONDON • NEW YORK • SYDNEY • CAPETOWN • MONTREAL

READER'S DIGEST NEEDLECRAFT GUIDE: CROCHET & LACEMAKING
First published 1995
Copyright © Text and Illustrations 1995, 1981

The material in this book first appeared in
READER'S DIGEST COMPLETE GUIDE TO NEEDLEWORK
First edition Copyright © 1981
Reprinted 1991
The Reader's Digest Association Limited,
Berkeley Square House, Berkeley Square, London W1X 6AB

Copyright © 1981 Reader's Digest Association Far East Limited
Philippines Copyright 1981 Reader's Digest Association Far East Ltd

Printed in Italy

ISBN 0 2764 2179 5

CONTRIBUTORS

The publishers would like to thank the following people for major contributions to this series.

Consultant editor Eirian Short

Editorial contributors and designers

Louise Amble   Peggy Bendel   Sherry De Leon   Rosemary Drysdale   Katherine Enzmann   Phoebe Fox   Zuelia Ann Hurt
Barbara H. Jacksier   Joyce D. Lee   Susanna E. Lewis   Claudia Librett   Victoria Mileti   Edna Adam Walker
Monna Weinman   Joanne Whitwell

Technical assistance

Elspeth Arnold   Lesley Arnold   Betty Beeby   Linda Blyer   Barbara Dawson   Janet Eaton   Charlotte Feng-Veshi
Sheila Gore   Jane Iles   Diana Keay   Elizabeth Kerr   Arlene Mintzer   Carole Nolan   Erwin Rowland
Cathie Strunz   Valentina Watson   Joan Webb

Contributing artists

Roberta W. Frauwirth   Susan Frye   Pat Kemmish   John A. Lind Corp.   Marilyn MacGregor   Mary Ruth Roby   Jim Silks
Randall Lieu   Ray Skibinski   Lynn E. Yost

Contributing photographers

J. D. Barnell   Bruton Photography   Joel Elkins   Ken Korsh   Ross McCann/Conrad-Dell-McCrann, Inc.   Michael A. Vaccaro

Research assistance

Aero Needles (Abel Morrall)   Appletons Bros Ltd   C. J. Bates & Son   Emile Bernat & Sons Co.   Bernina Sewing Machines
Boye Needle Company   Brunswick Worsted Mills Inc.   J. & P. Coats   Cowling & Wilcox   Craftsman's Mark
The D.M.C. Corporation   Embroiderers' Guild   Frederick J. Fawcett Inc.   T. Forsell & Son   Harrods Ltd
Harry M. Fraser Company   Hayfield Textiles   Hosiery Machine Co.   Kreinik Mfg Co.   Lowe & Carr   H. Milward & Sons
Newey Goodman   Paternayan Bros Inc.   Paton & Baldwins   Phildar International   Pingouin   Reynolds Yarn Inc.
Royal School of Needlework   Singer Company (UK) Ltd   Sirdar   Talon/Donahue Sales Div. of Textron   Joan Toggitt Ltd
Twilleys of Stamford   Vilene   Whitecroft Scovill   Wm E. Wright Co.

Cover

Photography by Paul Biddle   Craftwork supplied by Phyllis Meyrick (crochet) and Wendy Benson (lace)

Crochet

Crochet basics | **6**
Yarns, hooks, other equipment
Introduction to crocheting | 8
Holding the hook/Right-handed
Making the chain stitch/Right-handed
Holding the hook/Left-handed | 9
Making the chain stitch/Left-handed
Forming the elementary stitches | 10
Variations on elementary techniques | 12

Following crochet instructions | **14**
Testing the tension
Joining and securing yarns
Increasing and decreasing | 15
Geometric shapes | 16

Crochet stitches | **18**
Using a pattern stitch
Textures
Shells | 20
Clusters | 22
Motifs | 23
Motifs/Patchwork | 24
Meshes | 26
Shaping mesh ground | 27
Filet crochet | 28
Overlaid meshes | 29
Irish crochet | 30
Irish crochet cushion top | 31
Tunisian crochet | 32
Loops | 34
Multicolour stitches | 36
Working with a colour chart
Jacquard techniques
Charted stitches | 38

Crocheting a garment | **39**
Introduction
Designing a crocheted garment
Charting a woman's cardigan | 40
How to make a garment chart
Shaping necklines | 42
Shaping armholes and sleeves | 43
Ribbing | 44
Buttons
Buttonholes | 45

Assembling and finishing | **46**
Crocheted edgings and insertions | 47

Lacemaking | **49**
Index | **80**

Crochet basics

Yarns
Hooks and supplementary equipment
Holding the hook/Right-handed
Making the chain stitch/Right-handed
Holding the hook/Left-handed
Making the chain stitch/Left-handed
Forming the elementary stitches
Variations on elementary techniques

Yarns

Crocheting can be done with any stringy material from finest tatting cotton to raffia, leather cords or fabric strips. Your choice only has to suit the purpose and be worked with an appropriate hook (see opposite page for selection).

For convenience in comparing similar yarn types, a chart of wools and synthetic yarns appears on the opening page of the Knitting chapter; below is a chart of crochet yarns. A significant difference between these two groups: yarns in the first are sold by weight, those in the second by ball. Sometimes the length is shown in metres.

Most cotton yarns are *mercerised;* this means they have undergone a process that strengthens and gives them greater lustre. Most are *colourfast,* a term that signifies colours will not run or fade in hot water. Some of these terms appear on the label, along with other descriptive information, such as number of *plies* or *cords* – single units – that have been twisted together, and sometimes a number (usually between 10 and 60) that signifies thickness of the ply. The higher the number, the finer the yarn. If yarn comes in a skein, it is best to wind it in a ball to prevent it tangling in use.

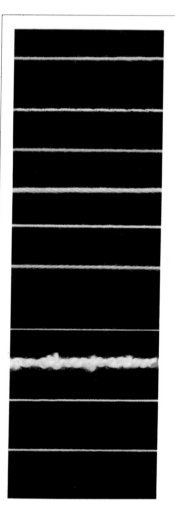

VARIETIES OF YARNS

Coloured crochet cotton, No. 5. This is a 4-ply, firmly twisted thread, made in a large selection of colours. It is suitable for making shawls, blouses, dresses, bedspreads, curtains and trimmings.

Metallic synthetic yarn, No. 5. This is a 4-ply synthetic yarn, bound with metallic thread, available in white and some colours. It is suitable for making sweaters, blouses and fashion accessories.

Crochet cotton, No. 5. This is a 4-ply, firmly twisted thread, made by a different manufacturer and slightly finer than the thread shown at the top of this table. It is suitable for making the same items.

Crochet cotton, No. 3. This is a 2-ply firmly twisted thread, made in a large selection of colours, and can be used to make place mats, tablecloths and bedspreads.

Crochet cotton, No. 5. This is a thread more firmly twisted and slightly finer than the other No. 5 threads shown in this table. It is very suitable for bedspreads, tablecloths, place mats and trimmings.

Pearl cotton, No. 5. This 2-ply thread is very loosely twisted and has a high sheen. It is made in a large selection of colours and is suitable for clothes, trimmings and fashion accessories.

Tatting thread, No. 60. This is a 6-ply cotton thread, very firmly twisted, and is made in several colours. It is used for tatting, lacemaking and for crochet trimmings.

Bouclé yarn. This is made in various thicknesses, and is mostly 3-ply. It is a loosely twisted slubbed yarn suitable for sweaters, dresses and fashion accessories.

Crochet cotton, No. 20 and 30. This is a 6-ply, fine firmly twisted thread, mostly available in pale shades and suitable for lace, trimmings and delicate crochet tablecloths and mats.

Crochet cotton, No. 10, 20, 30 and 40. This is a 6-ply, fine firmly twisted thread available in many thicknesses and colours and suitable for trimmings, lace, place mats and tablecloths.

Hooks and supplementary equipment

Crochet hooks are made in many sizes and materials. Thickness of most hooks is indicated by a number (the number corresponds to the same size in a knitting needle); the larger the number, the larger the size. Steel hooks for fine crochet are usually 13 cm long, and made in a range of sizes from 60 mm to 1.75 mm. When selecting a hook, the thicker your yarn, the larger your hook should be to make the work easier.

Collect several sizes of crochet hook, so that if the tension of a sample is not right you can make another sample using a hook that is one size larger or smaller.

To prevent the hooks getting lost, keep them together with an elastic band in your work-basket, or if you prefer, make a felt bag with a narrow pocket for each hook, like a pencil case. Mark each section with the size of the hook and it will be easy to keep the hooks safe, and to find a hook quickly to use for any piece of crochet.

The illustration below shows two hooks – the fine steel hook and the normal hook that are available from most shops. The others are more unusual, but are included for general interest. Most hooks are made of aluminium, but wood or plastic hooks make a change to work with.

There are supplementary knitting aids available that can be useful for crochet. Among these are row counters to keep track of the work completed, coiled ring markers, a ruler for measuring tension, and also a gauge for measuring hook sizes.

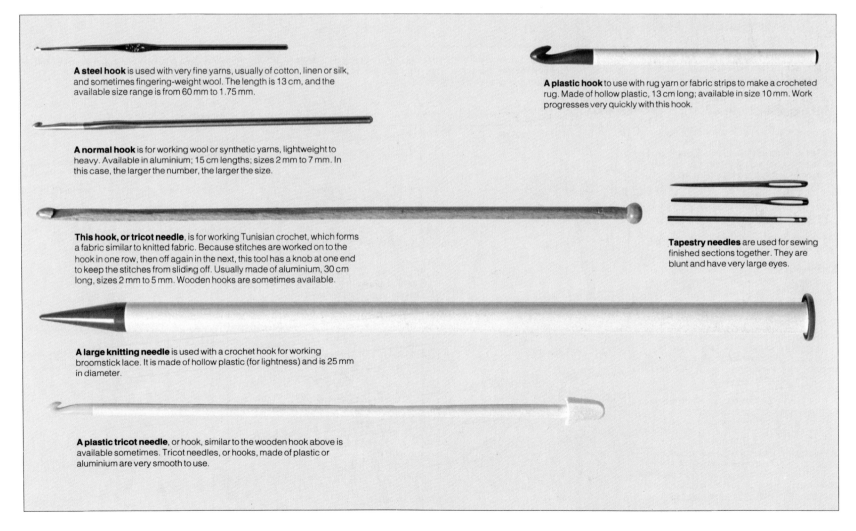

A steel hook is used with very fine yarns, usually of cotton, linen or silk, and sometimes fingering-weight wool. The length is 13 cm, and the available size range is from 60 mm to 1.75 mm.

A normal hook is for working wool or synthetic yarns, lightweight to heavy. Available in aluminium; 15 cm lengths; sizes 2 mm to 7 mm. In this case, the larger the number, the larger the size.

This hook, or tricot needle, is for working Tunisian crochet, which forms a fabric similar to knitted fabric. Because stitches are worked on to the hook in one row, then off again in the next, this tool has a knob at one end to keep the stitches from sliding off. Usually made of aluminium, 30 cm long, sizes 2 mm to 5 mm. Wooden hooks are sometimes available.

A large knitting needle is used with a crochet hook for working broomstick lace. It is made of hollow plastic (for lightness) and is 25 mm in diameter.

A plastic tricot needle, or hook, similar to the wooden hook above is available sometimes. Tricot needles, or hooks, made of plastic or aluminium are very smooth to use.

A plastic hook to use with rug yarn or fabric strips to make a crocheted rug. Made of hollow plastic, 13 cm long; available in size 10 mm. Work progresses very quickly with this hook.

Tapestry needles are used for sewing finished sections together. They are blunt and have very large eyes.

Crochet basics

Introduction to crocheting

All crochet stitches are formed by inter-locking loops. The basic stitch is the chain stitch, shown below. To work a chain, the hook is held in one hand and yarn is held taut in the other, while the hand holding the yarn also supports the work where the hook enters it.

Two common ways to hold a hook with the right hand are shown on the immediate right. Use whichever feels more comfortable. There are several correct methods of holding yarn; one is illustrated below. The basic idea is to keep the yarn taut over your index finger so you can manipulate it easily and with even tension around the hook.

Holding the hook/Right-handed

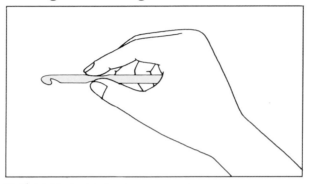

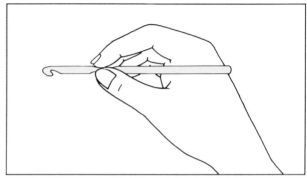

Method 1. With hook facing down, grasp tool in the right hand, holding it almost as you would a knife, with thumb and index finger on either side of the flat part, middle finger resting against the thumb.

Method 2. With hook facing down, grasp tool in the right hand, holding it as you would a pencil, with thumb and index finger on either side of the flat part, middle finger resting against the thumb.

Making the chain stitch/Right-handed

The chain stitch (ch) is used to form the first row of crochet, and is an integral part of many pattern stitches as well. As the foundation, it should be formed loosely enough for the hook to enter each chain easily, without drawing in the edge of the work.

1. To start chain, make a slip knot about 15 cm from the yarn end; insert hook right to left.

2. Pulling both yarn ends, draw in the loop until it is close to hook, but not too tight.

3. Wrap ball end of yarn around little finger of left hand, take it under fourth and third fingers, then over top of index finger, leaving about 5 cm of yarn between finger and hook.

4. Holding the slip knot between thumb and middle finger of left hand, and keeping yarn taut over index finger, push hook forward, at the same time twisting it, so yarn passes over it back to front and is caught in the slot.

5. Draw yarn through the loop, thus forming a new loop on the hook. The newly formed loop should be loose enough for the next chain to be drawn through it easily.

6. Holding chain nearest the hook with thumb and middle finger, repeat Steps 4 and 5 until you have desired number of chains (loop on hook does not count as part of the total). All chains should be the same size. If they are not, it is best to pull them out and start again.

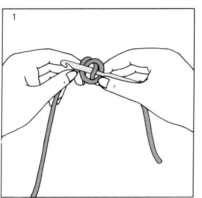

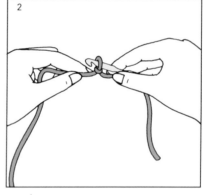

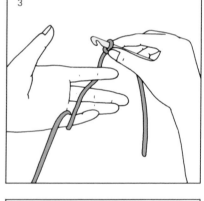

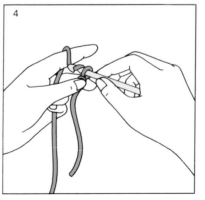

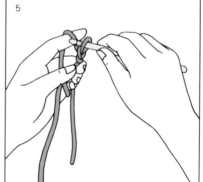

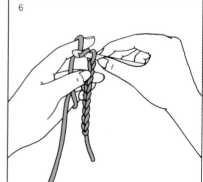

Holding the hook/Left-handed

Crocheting with the left hand is exactly the same as with the right hand, but with the hook and yarn position reversed. Because starting a new technique can be difficult if you have to mirror illustrations, instructions on this page are provided to help the left-handed person.

Two common ways to hold a hook with the left hand are shown on the immediate right. Use whichever feels more comfortable. There are several correct methods of holding yarn; one is illustrated below. The basic idea is to keep the yarn taut over your index finger so you can manipulate it easily and with even tension around the hook.

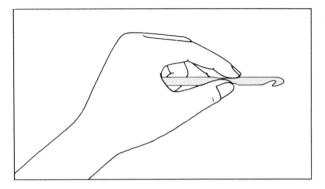

Method 1. With hook facing down, grasp tool in the left hand, holding it almost as you would a knife, with thumb and index finger on either side of the flat part, middle finger resting against the thumb.

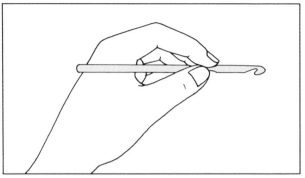

Method 2. With hook facing down, grasp tool in the left hand, holding it as you would a pencil, with thumb and index finger on either side of the flat part, middle finger resting against the thumb.

Making the chain stitch/Left-handed

The chain stitch (ch) is used to form the first row of crochet, and is an integral part of many pattern stitches as well. As the foundation, it should be formed loosely enough for the hook to enter each chain easily, without drawing in the edge of the work.

1. To start chain, make a slip knot about 15 cm from the yarn end; insert hook left to right.

2. Pulling both yarn ends, draw in the loop until it is close to hook, but not too tight.

3. Wrap ball end of yarn around little finger of right hand, take it under fourth and third fingers, then over top of index finger, leaving about 5 cm of yarn between finger and hook.

4. Holding the slip knot between thumb and middle finger of right hand, and keeping yarn taut over the index finger, push hook forward, at the same time twisting it, so yarn passes over it back to front and is caught in the slot.

5. Draw yarn through the loop, thus forming a new loop on the hook. The newly formed loop should be loose enough for the next chain to be drawn through it easily.

6. Holding chain nearest the hook with thumb and middle finger, repeat Steps 4 and 5 until you have desired number of chains (loop on hook does not count as part of the total). All chains should be the same size. If they are not, it is best to pull them out and start again.

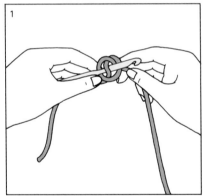

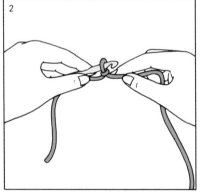

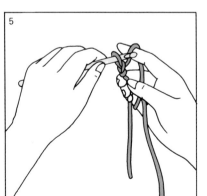

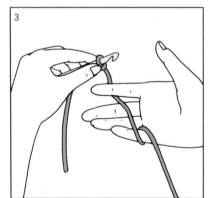

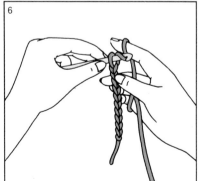

Crochet basics

Forming the elementary stitches

Double crochet (dc). Shortest of the basic stitches, it makes a firm, flat fabric. Often used to finish edges of other stitch patterns, and sometimes to join two finished sections.

Insert hook in 2nd chain from hook, catch yarn (A), and draw a loop through the chain (2 loops on hook), yarn round hook and draw through 2 loops to complete stitch (B). Work 1 double crochet in each chain across row. After last stitch, work 1 chain and turn; insert hook in 1st stitch to start next row (C).

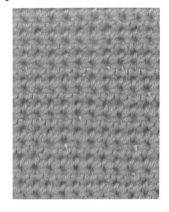

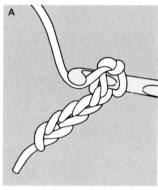

Insert hook in 2nd ch

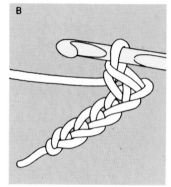

Double crochet stitch completed

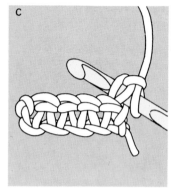

1 ch to turn, insert hook in 1st st

Half treble crochet (htr). Slightly taller than double crochet, this stitch has a pronounced ridge in its texture; makes a firm, attractive fabric.

Yarn round hook and insert hook in 3rd chain from hook, catch yarn (A) and draw a loop through the chain (3 loops on hook), yarn round hook, draw a loop through 3 loops to complete stitch (B). Work 1 half treble crochet in each chain across the row. After last stitch, work 2 chain and turn; yarn round hook, insert hook in 1st stitch to start next row (C).

Insert hook in 3rd chain

Half treble crochet stitch completed

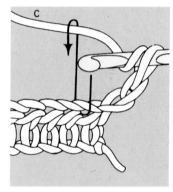

2 ch to turn, insert hook in 1st st

Treble crochet (tr). Twice as tall as double crochet and less compact. Forms the basis of many pattern stitches.

Yarn round hook and insert hook in 4th chain from hook, catch yarn (A), draw a loop through the chain (3 loops on hook), yarn round hook, draw through 2 loops, yarn round hook, draw through last 2 loops to complete stitch (B). Make 1 treble crochet in each chain across the row. After last stitch, work 3 chain and turn; yarn round hook, insert hook in 2nd stitch for next row (C).

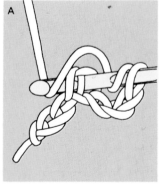

Yarn round hook, insert hook in 4th ch

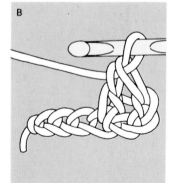

Treble crochet stitch completed

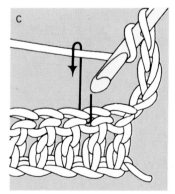

3 ch to turn, insert hook in 2nd st

Double treble crochet (dtr).

A tall stitch, more open than treble crochet and used less frequently.

Yarn round hook twice, insert hook in 5th chain from hook, catch yarn (A), draw a loop through the chain (4 loops on hook), yarn round hook, draw through 2 loops, yarn round hook, yarn round hook, draw through 2 loops, yarn round hook, draw through last 2 loops to complete stitch (B). Work 1 double treble crochet in each chain across row, 4 chain, turn, yarn round hook twice, insert hook in 2nd stitch to start next row (C).

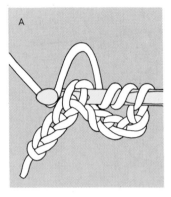
Yarn round hook twice, insert in 5th ch

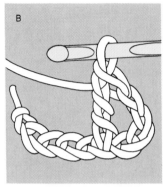
Double treble crochet stitch completed

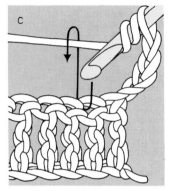
4 ch to turn, insert hook in 2nd st

Triple treble crochet (trtr).

Essentially the same as double treble but taller. You can make an even taller stitch by adding yet another loop of yarn round the hook at the beginning.

Yarn round hook 3 times, insert hook in 6th ch from hook, catch yarn (A), draw a loop through chain (5 loops on hook), *yarn round hook, draw through 2 loops*, repeat the instructions between *3 more times to complete stitch (B). Make 1 triple treble crochet in each chain across row, 5 chain, turn; yarn round hook 3 times, insert hook in 2nd stitch to start next row (C).

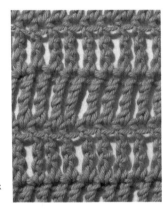

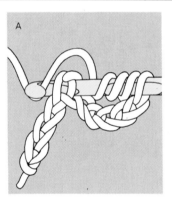
Yarn round hook 3 times, insert in 6th ch

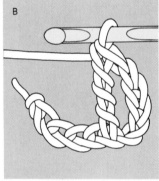
Triple treble crochet stitch completed

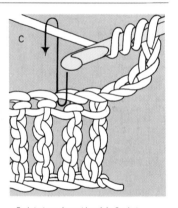
5 ch to turn, insert hook in 2nd st

Slipstitch (ss).

A very short stitch used primarily for joining, as in the closing of a ring or motif round, or the seaming of two finished pieces. Though not used to produce fabric, it is sometimes worked along an edge to strengthen it and to minimise stretching.

Insert hook in chain (or stitch), catch yarn (A), draw a loop through both the chain and the loop on the hook (B).

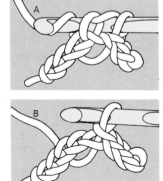

BASIC CROCHET RULES

1. The chain on the hook is never counted as part of a foundation row. For example, if directions say 18 chain, you should have 18 in addition to one on the hook.
2. Always insert hook into a chain or stitch from front to back.*
3. Always insert hook under the two top loops of a chain or stitch.*
4. There should be just one loop left on the hook at completion of a stitch or sequence.

*Unless directions say otherwise.

TURNING CHAINS

At the beginning of each row (including the first one) a certain number of chains are needed to bring work up to the level of the stitch that is to be formed. The exact number of chains depends on the height of the stitch (see below), and in the case of tall stitches – treble, double treble, and so on – this chain usually replaces the first stitch of each row. When instructions place the turning chain at the end of a row, you should turn work right to left to avoid twisting the chain, then insert hook in the stitch that is specified.

Stitch	Turning chains
Double crochet	1 chain to turn, insert hook in 1st stitch
Half treble crochet	2 chains to turn, insert hook in 1st stitch
Treble crochet	3 chains to turn, insert hook in 2nd stitch
Double treble crochet	4 chains to turn, insert hook in 2nd stitch
Triple treble crochet	5 chains to turn, insert hook in 2nd stitch

Crochet basics

Variations on elementary techniques

Working under one loop produces a ribbed effect and a more open pattern than is achieved with the usual technique (that is, inserting the hook under two loops).
To work the back loop only, insert hook front to back with a downward motion, catch the yarn (A), draw up a loop and complete the stitch.
To work the front loop only, insert hook front to back with an upward motion, catch the yarn (B), draw up a loop and complete the stitch.

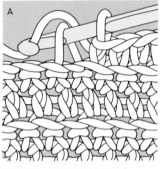

Working a stitch in back loop only

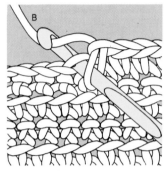

Working a stitch in front loop only

Working between stitches is a technique used in many patterns, meshes (p. 26), for example. One or more chains are made between stitches in one row; in the next row, you crochet into the *chain* or *chain space*. Always note which method is specified, because results are different for each.
To work into chain between stitches, insert hook under the 2 top loops; make stitch *through* the chain (A).
To work into a chain space between stitches, insert hook under the chain and make a stitch or group of stitches *over* the chain (B).

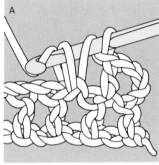

Working *into* chain between stitches

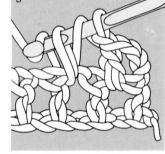

Working *over* chain between stitches

Raised stitches use a technique that creates a three-dimensional effect. Though it is shown here applied to treble crochet, the method is suitable also for double or double treble crochet. The raised stitches can be worked to either the front or the back, or alternately front and back, depending on the desired results. See p. 19 for patterns in which this technique is employed.

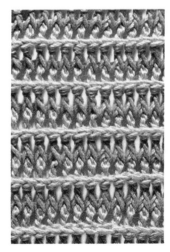

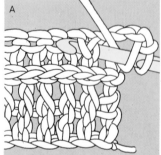

Raised treble round the front. Yarn round hook, insert hook front to back between next 2 stitches, then bring it forward between the stitch being worked and the one after it; hook is now positioned horizontally behind stitch. Complete the treble crochet.

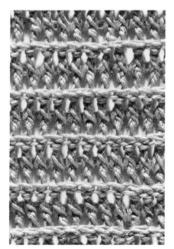

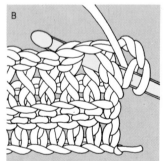

Raised treble round the back. Yarn round hook, insert hook back to front between next 2 stitches, then back again between the stitch being worked and the one after it; hook is now positioned horizontally in front of stitch. Complete the treble crochet.

A double chain stitch makes a sturdier foundation than a simple chain. It can also be used alone for a narrow trimming or cord.

Make a slip knot and 2 chain, work 1 double crochet in 2nd chain from hook, *insert hook under the left loop of the double crochet, catch yarn (A) and draw up a loop (B), yarn round hook, draw through 2 loops (C)*. Repeat instructions between asterisks until chain is the desired length.

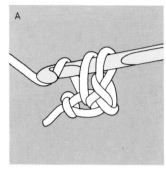

Working under left loop of the dc

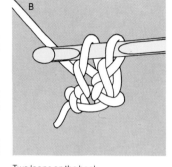

Two loops on the hook

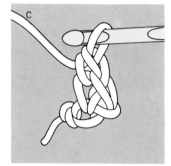

Loop drawn through the 2 loops

Double-faced treble crochet makes a sturdy, very thick fabric. *Multiple of any number of chains*
Row 1: *1 treble crochet in each chain*, 3 chain, turn
Row 2: With fabric sideways, miss 1st stitch, *yarn round hook, insert hook in back loop of next stitch and back loop of foundation chain, catch yarn (A), draw a loop through 2 back loops, then complete treble crochet (B)*, repeat from asterisk to end of row, 3 chain, turn. Repeat Row 2, working into back of each treble crochet on this and previous row (C).

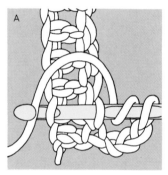

Working under 2 back loops of Row 1

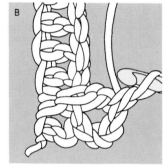

A treble crochet completed in Row 2

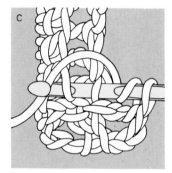

Starting the 1st stitch of Row 3

Solomon's knot is a double knot stitch. The elongated loops are interlocked in such a way that they produce a mesh fabric similar to netting. Though 1.5 cm is the typical recommendation for loop length in many instructions, any length is suitable so long as it is consistent. A general rule is to make a longer loop for a thick yarn, a shorter loop for a fine one. As you follow the directions, right, for forming a single knot, pay close attention to where the hook is inserted after a chain is drawn through the long loop (illustration A); correct insertion of the hook in this step is important to obtain the desired result.

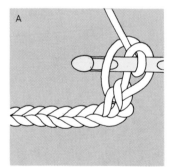

Work 1 double crochet in the 2nd chain from the hook, *lengthen loop on hook to 1.5 cm, draw up new loop, take hook across front of elongated loop and insert it under the yarn that was drawn up for the new loop (A), work 1 double crochet* to complete single knot.

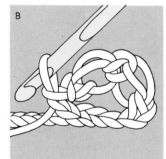

Repeat instructions between asterisks and you will have made a *double knot*. *Miss 3 chains, work 1 double crochet in next chain (B), make 1 double knot.* Repeat instructions between these last 2 asterisks across the row, ending with 3 single knot stitches.

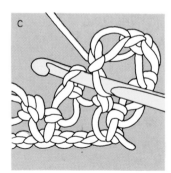

Turn, *work 1 double crochet in centre of next double knot (C), make 1 double knot.* Repeat instructions between the last 2 asterisks across the row, ending with 1 single knot. This row is repeated to form a pattern (see p. 27 for an example of the finished stitch).

Following crochet instructions

Crochet terms
Testing the tension
Joining and finishing yarn ends
Increasing
Decreasing
Geometric shapes worked in rows
Working in rounds

ch	chain pp. 8–9
ss	slipstitch p. 11
dc	double crochet p. 10
htr	half treble crochet p. 10
tr	treble crochet p. 10
dtr	double treble crochet p. 11
trtr	triple treble p. 11
alt	alternate
beg	begin, beginning
dec	decrease pp. 15–16
inc	increase p. 15
patt	pattern
rep	repeat
rnd	round p. 17
tog	together
st	stitch
sp	space
yrh	yarn round hook

*	*	Instructions between asterisks are repeated until the number of stitches specified runs out
(	)	Steps within parentheses are worked according to instructions that follow the parenthesis, either worked into one stitch, or repeated a specified number of times
[	]	Instructions in brackets explain a particular stitch or technique
tension		The number of stitches and rows per cm
mark stitch		Tie on contrasting yarn or slip a coil ring marker on the stitch indicated
unit		The number of stitches required to work one repeat of a pattern stitch
work straight		Continue to work pattern without increasing or decreasing

Crochet terminology

For written crochet instructions, there is a special vocabulary, much of it expressed in abbreviated or symbolic form. The forms used in this book are listed below with their definition. Also included are the numbers of pages on which techniques are illustrated. You may encounter slight variations of the terms given here, but these are common British forms. Before using new instructions, you should find out whether they are British or American, because American terms have different meanings. Our double crochet, for example, is the same as American single crochet.

An alternative to written instructions is a chart. For this purpose, different symbols are used (see pp. 302 and 304).

Testing the tension

All crochet instructions have a specified tension – the number of stitches that equals 5 cm. Some also include row tension – the number of rows to 5 cm. Because the size of a finished piece is based on these calculations, it is important to get the tension right before proceeding with any new project.

For a test sample, make a chain 10 cm in length, using the specified yarn and hook size. Work in pattern until the pattern measures 10 cm; fasten off. Measure the tension as shown on the right. If an adjustment is necessary, make a new sample using a hook either one size larger or smaller.

To measure stitch tension, insert two pins, 5 cm apart; count stitches between. If pin falls in centre of a stitch, tension may be measured over 10 cm.

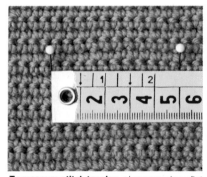

To measure stitch tension, place sample on flat surface; insert two pins, 5 cm apart; count stitches between them. If pin falls in centre of a stitch, tension may be measured over 10 cm.

TO JOIN AND SECURE YARNS

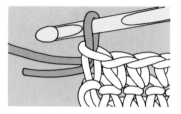

To join a new yarn at the end of a row, work last stitch with first yarn to final 2 loops; draw up last loop with new yarn.

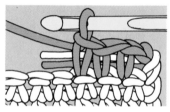

Cut first yarn to 5 cm. Make a chain; turn. Pull up 2 short yarns and lay over previous row; work over them for 4-5 stitches.

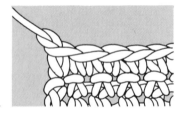

To secure yarn end on a finished piece, cut yarn to a 15 cm length; pull this end through the last loop and tighten it.

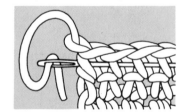

Thread yarn end in tapestry or rug needle; weave into back of work for 2 to 5 cm, below top row of stitches. Cut remainder.

Following crochet instructions

Shaping

Shaping in crochet is done by increasing and decreasing. Once mastered, these techniques permit you to crochet any shape or form. Six examples are shown overleaf, more on p. 17.

A single increase is made by working twice into the same stitch. If made within a row, and repeated over several rows, the increase positions move right or left. To keep the progression orderly, place a marker (contrasting yarn or a plastic coil ring) where increasing begins. For shaping to the right, increase before the marker; to the left, after the marker. On the next row, reverse this order to maintain consistency of the direction.

A single decrease is made by working two successive stitches into one final loop. Repeated over several rows, progression is the same as for increasing.

Increasing

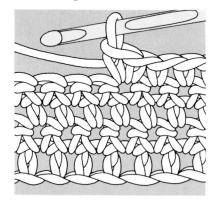

To make a single increase, work 2 stitches in 1 stitch. Double crochet is shown in the example; all other stitches are increased the same way.

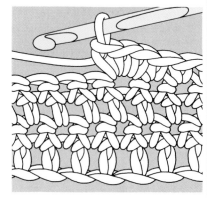

To make a double increase, work 3 stitches in 1 stitch. Double crochet is shown in the example; all other stitches are increased the same way.

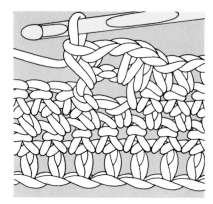

To make a decorative double increase (lacy chevron), work 2 chains at increase point. On next and subsequent rows, work (1 stitch, 2 chains, 1 stitch) in 2-chain space of previous row.

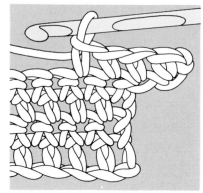

To increase several stitches at one edge, as when a sleeve is made in one piece with the garment, extend a chain from the side edge, then work back along the chain on the next row.

Decreasing

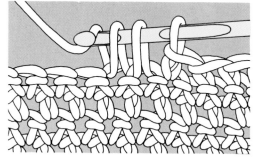

To decrease 1 stitch in double or half treble crochet, insert hook in stitch, draw up a loop, insert hook in next stitch, draw up a loop (3 loops on hook), yarn round hook, draw through the 3 loops.

If a decrease occurs at the beginning of a row, you can, if you prefer, miss the first stitch instead of working 2 stitches together. If a decrease is designated for the end of a row, miss the next to last stitch.

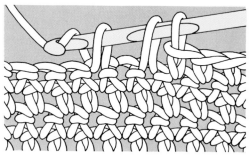

To decrease 2 stitches in double or half treble crochet, insert hook in stitch, draw up a loop, miss next stitch, insert hook in next stitch, draw up a loop (there are 3 loops on the hook, as shown), yarn round hook, draw through the 3 loops.

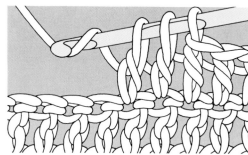

To decrease 1 stitch in treble crochet, yarn round hook, insert hook in stitch, draw up a loop, yarn round hook, draw through 2 loops, yarn round hook, insert hook in next stitch, draw up a loop, yarn round hook, draw through 2 loops (3 loops on hook), yarn round hook, draw through 3 loops.

If a decrease occurs at beginning of a row, you can miss the first stitch instead of working 2 stitches together; if at end of a row, miss next to last stitch.

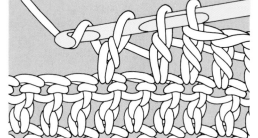

To decrease 2 stitches in treble crochet, yarn round hook, insert hook in stitch, draw up a loop, yarn round hook, draw through 2 loops, miss next stitch, yarn round hook, insert hook in next stitch, draw up a loop, yarn round hook, draw through 2 loops (there are 3 loops on the hook, as shown), yarn round hook, draw through 3 loops.

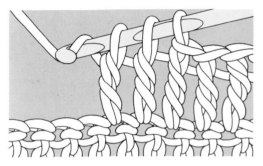

To decrease 1 stitch in double treble crochet, yarn round hook twice, insert hook in stitch, draw up a loop, yarn round hook, draw through 2 loops, yarn round hook, draw through 2 loops (2 loops remain on hook); yarn round hook twice, insert hook in next stitch, draw up a loop, yarn round hook, draw through 2 loops, yarn round hook, draw through 2 loops (there are 3 loops on the hook, as shown), yarn round hook, draw through last 3 loops.

To decrease 2 stitches in double treble crochet, follow the method for decreasing 1 stitch, but miss a stitch between the 2 stitches that are worked together.

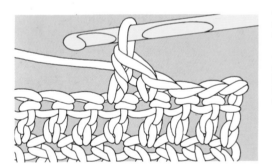

To decrease several stitches at the beginning of a row without an abrupt change in stitch heights, omit turning chain and work slipstitches for the number of decreases, make 1 double crochet in next stitch, then continue in pattern. Do not work the slipstitches on return row.

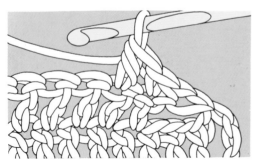

To decrease several stitches at the end of a row without an abrupt change in stitch heights, leave unworked the number of stitches to be decreased, work 1 slipstitch at end of row, 1 chain and turn. Miss the slipstitch, work 1 double crochet in the next stitch, then continue in pattern.

Geometric shapes/Worked in rows

Oval. Stitches worked around the chain instead of back and forth.
6 ch
Row 1: miss 1 ch, 1 dc in each of next 4 ch, 3 dc in last ch, turn work so bottom of ch is on top.
Row 2: 1 dc in each of next 5 ch (working into single loop that remains after working Row 1), 3 dc into ch that was missed in Row 1, continue around, working next row in sts of Row 1.
Row 3: *1 dc in each st*, 2 dc in last st, 2 dc in end st, 2 dc in st that begins row on opposite side. Continue as in Row 3, increasing stitches at ends as needed.

Triangle. Formed by increasing the first and last stitches every other row. The triangle becomes a diamond if, after reaching the desired width, you continue in pattern, decreasing the first and last stitches on alternate rows.
2 ch
Row 1: 1 dc, turn.
Row 2: 3 dc in the 1 dc, ch 1, turn.
Row 3: 2 dc in 1st dc, 1 in each of next 2 dc, 2 dc in last dc, 1 ch, turn.
Row 4: *1 dc in each dc*, ch 1, turn.
Row 5: 2 dc in 1st dc, *1 sc in next dc*, 2 dc in last dc, ch 1, turn.
Continue increasing in this manner until desired size is reached; fasten off.

Square. Formed by working increases in the centre stitch of each row. An attractive variation on the usual approach, which is to work a square in straight rows.
2 ch
Row 1: 3 dc in 2nd ch from hook, 1 ch, turn.
Row 2: 1 dc in 1st st, 3 dc in next st, 1 dc in last st, 1 ch, turn.
Row 3: 1 dc in each of 1st 2 sts, 3 dc in next st, 1 dc in each of last 2 sts, 1 ch, turn.
Row 4: 1 dc in each of 1st 3 sts, 3 dc in next st, 1 dc in each of last 3 sts, 1 ch, turn.
Continue as in Row 4, working 1 dc in each st except the centre one, in which you work 3 dc.

Following crochet instructions

Geometric shapes/ Worked in rounds

Crocheting in rounds is an alternative to working in rows. Flat geometric shapes, also bowl and tube shapes, are formed in this way. Each is started with a ring (see method below), and is then developed in either concentric or spiral rounds, always working from the right side. For concentric shaping, each round is started with a chain, which acts as a substitute for the first stitch, and ends with a slipstitch into the starting chain (see illustration D, below). Examples of a concentric approach are the geometric shapes, right, and patchwork motifs, pp. 24–25. Angles on motifs are formed with increases of two or four stitches placed directly above one another.

In spiral shaping, each round continues out of the previous one, with no starting chain or closing slipstitch. For this method, you should place a marker at the end of Round 1, then move it up with each new round to keep track of the rounds completed. For smooth shaping, the position of increases or decreases is usually moved forward by one stitch on each round. The hats, opposite, are typical examples of this technique.

A tube is also made in spiral fashion. To form a tube, you start with a ring of the desired diameter, then keep working around it (usually with double crochet), neither increasing nor decreasing, until the tube is as long as you wish.

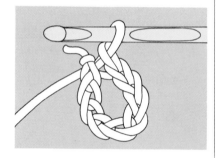

To form ring, make a chain; join last chain to first with a slipstitch (A and B). Depending on how large you want the centre space to be, allow 1 chain for every 2 to 4 stitches of first round.

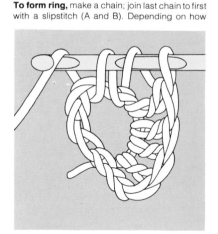

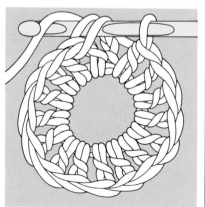

To work the first (centre) round, start with a chain or stitch, as directed, and work stitches over the ring (C); for concentric rounds, close with a slipstitch in top of first chain (D).

Circle. Concentric rounds worked with enough increases to keep edges from curling. The number and placing of increases may have to be adjusted for a particular yarn, hook size or stitch that is used, but a general formula is to increase each round by the number of sts that you started with.
6 ch and join in a ring with ss
Round 1: 3 ch, 11 tr in ring, ss in top of beg ch (total of 12 sts).
Round 2: 3 ch, 1 tr in ss, 2 tr in each tr of Round 1, ss in top of beg ch (24 sts).
Round 3: 3 ch, 2 tr in next tr, (1 tr in next tr, 2 tr in next tr) 11 times, ss in top of beg ch (36 sts).
To continue, increase in every 3rd st on **Round 4,** every 4th st on **Round 5,** and so on, increasing by 12 stitches on every round.

Square. Sample (left) is in treble crochet, but any stitch is suitable, as long as number of stitches in Round 1 is divisible by 4.
6 ch and join in a ring with ss
Round 1: 3 ch, 2 tr in ring, 1 ch, (3 tr in ring, 1 ch) 3 times, ss in top of beg ch (total of 12 sts).
Round 2: 3 ch, 1 tr in each of next 2 sts, *(2 tr, 1 ch, 2 tr) in ch sp, 1 tr in each of next 3 sts*, (2 tr, 1 ch, 2 tr) in last ch sp, ss in top of beg ch (28 sts).
Round 3: 3 ch, 1 tr in each of next 4 sts, *(2 tr, 1 ch, 2 tr) in ch sp, 1 tr in each of next 7 sts*, (2 tr, 1 ch, 2 tr) in last ch sp, 1 tr in each of next 2 sts, ss in top of beg ch (44 sts).
Continue evenly along each side, working (2 tr, 1 ch, 2 tr) in the ch sp at each corner, increasing 16 sts on each round.

Octagon. Structured same as a square, but with 2 increases in each angle instead of 4 (to keep it flat). Number of stitches in Round 1 is divisible by number of sides.
4 ch and join in a ring with ss
Round 1: 2 ch, 1 htr in ring, 1 ch, (2 htr in ring, 1 ch) 7 times, ss in top of beg ch (total of 16 sts).
Round 2: 2 ch, 1 htr in next st, *(1 htr, 1 ch, 1 htr) in ch sp, 1 htr in each of next 2 sts*, (1 htr, 1 ch, 1 htr) in last ch sp, ss in top of beg ch (32 sts).
Round 3: 2 ch, 1 htr in each of next 3 sts, *(1 htr, 1 ch, 1 htr) in ch sp, 1 htr in each of next 4 sts*, (1 htr, 1 ch, 1 htr) in last ch sp, ss in top of beg ch (48 sts).
Continue evenly along each side, working (1 htr, 1 ch, 1 htr) in each angle, increasing 16 sts on each round.

Crochet stitches

Selecting a pattern stitch
Textures
Shells
Clusters
Motifs
Motifs/Patchwork
Meshes
Shaping mesh ground
Filet crochet
Overlaid meshes
Irish crochet
Tunisian crochet
Loop stitches
Multicolour crochet
Charting a pattern stitch

Selecting a pattern stitch

A **pattern stitch** is a sequence of crochet techniques, repeated continuously to form a fabric. There are two ways of working a pattern – in *rows* or in *rounds*.

To work a pattern in rows, start with a number of chains which is a multiple of the stitches needed to complete one horizontal motif, plus any additional chains indicated. These extra chains include the ones that will be missed at the beginning of Row 1, and sometimes a few for balancing pattern motifs. (The chain on the hook is never counted.) After completing all rows in the pattern, begin again, usually at Row 2; the first row is usually a setting-up row. If a pattern is complex, use a row counter or markers to keep count.

To work a pattern in rounds, begin with a ring of chain stitches or yarn and work the first round into the ring (see p. 17 for the method). All subsequent rounds are worked with the right side facing you; the item is complete when you have obtained the desired size. It is not necessary to work all rounds.

Whether worked in rounds or rows, there is usually little difference between the two sides of a crochet pattern. Exceptions are some Tunisian stitches, also two-colour patterns in which yarn is carried up one side. Unless directions specify otherwise, Row 1 begins the right side.

Most pattern stitches can be classified according to structure. Familiarity with these basic structures will permit you to 'read' almost any pattern from a picture or sample. Patterns in this section are grouped according to type, though in some cases a stitch fits more than one category. The first group, *textures,* is a selection of compact patterns that are variations of basic crochet stitches. They are firmer and stiffer than the comparable knitted stitches. In selecting a pattern, consider its suitability for both yarn and purpose. Make a test sample to find out.

Textures

Alternate stitch. Two double crochets worked in every other stitch yield a firm fabric with leaf-like motif.
Unit of 2 ch plus 2
Row 1: miss 3 ch, 2 dc in next ch, *miss 1 ch, 2 dc in next ch*, 2 ch, turn
Row 2: *miss 1 st, 2 dc in next st*, 2 ch, turn
Rep from Row 2

Double stitch. Each stitch spans two.
Unit of 2 ch plus 2
Row 1: miss 2 ch, 1 double st [insert hook in next ch, yrh, draw through a loop, insert hook in next ch, yrh, draw through a loop, yrh, draw through 3 loops], *1 double st, inserting hook first in st where 2nd yrh was made for previous double st*, 2 ch, turn
Row 2: *1 double st in each pair of sts*, 1 double st inserting hook in last st and top of ch at beg, 2 ch, turn
Rep from Row 2

Up and down stitch. A varied texture produced by alternating double and treble crochet stitches.
Unit of 2 ch plus 2
Row 1: miss 2 ch, 1 dc in next ch, *1 tr, 1 dc*, 1 tr, 2 ch, turn
Row 2: miss 1st tr, *1 tr in dc of previous row, 1 dc in tr of previous row*, 1 tr in 2 ch of previous row, 2 ch, turn
Rep from Row 2

Chequerboard. Alternating bands of double and treble crochet stitches.
Unit of 10 ch plus 6
Row 1: miss 2 ch, 4 dc, *5 tr, 5 dc*, 3 ch, turn
Row 2: miss 1st st, 4 tr, *5 dc, 5 tr*, work last tr in top of ch at beginning of previous row, 2 ch, turn
Row 3: miss 1st st, 4 dc, *5 tr, 5 dc*, work last dc in top of turning ch, 3 ch, turn
Rep from Row 2

Woven stitch. Double crochet stitches worked in single chain spaces.
Unit of 3 ch plus 3
Row 1: miss 2 ch, 1 dc, *1 ch, miss 1 ch, 1 dc*, 2 ch, turn
Row 2: *1 dc in ch sp of previous row, 1 ch*, 1 dc in the turning ch sp, 2 ch, turn
Rep from Row 2

Crossed stitches. Treble crochet stitches worked in reverse order.
Unit of 3 ch plus 2
Row 1. miss 6 ch, 1 tr in next ch, 1 ch, 1 tr in 4th ch from beginning (crossing over the 1st tr tr), *miss 2 ch, 1 tr, 1 ch, 1 tr in 1st of missed ch*, 1 tr in last ch, 4 ch, turn
Row 2: miss 2 tr, 1 tr in next tr, 1 ch, 1 tr in last missed tr, *miss 1 tr, 1 tr in next tr, 1 ch, 1 tr in missed tr*, 1 tr in 3rd ch of turning ch, 4 ch, turn
Rep from Row 2

Diagonal stitch. Long stitch pulled diagonally across each group of three.
Unit of 4 ch plus 1
Row 1: miss 1 ch, *1 dc in each ch*, 2 ch, turn
Row 2: *miss 1 st, 1 tr in each of next 3 sts, insert hook in last missed st, yrh, draw through an elongated loop, yrh, draw through 2 loops*, 1 tr in last st, 1 ch, turn
Row 3: miss 1 st, *1 dc in each st*, 1 dc in turning ch, 2 ch, turn
Rep from Row 2

Open ridge stitch. A firm and heavy, yet airy pattern; especially suitable for a place mat or handbag.
Unit of 2 ch plus 1
Row 1: miss 1 ch, *1 dc in each ch*, 1 ch, turn
Row 2: 1 htr, *miss 1 st, 1 htr in next st, 1 htr between 2 preceding htr*; miss 1 st, 1 htr in ch at beg of row, 1 ch, turn
Row 3: *1 dc, inserting hook through back loop only of each st in previous row*, 1 ch; turn
Rep from Row 2

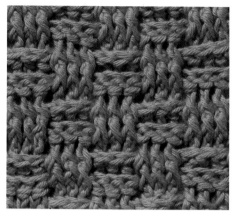

Basket weave. An unusual dimension is created by working raised stitches, first to the front, then the back. (See p. 276 for this technique.)
Unit of 6 ch
Row 1: miss 6 ch, *1 tr in next ch*, 2 ch, turn
Rows 2 and 3: miss 1 tr, *(1 raised tr round front) 3 times, (1 raised tr round back) 3 times*, (1 raised tr round front) 3 times, 1 tr in top of turning ch, 2 ch, turn
Rows 4 and 5: miss 1 tr, *(1 raised tr round back) 3 times, (1 raised tr round front) 3 times*, (1 raised tr round back) 3 times, 1 tr in top of turning ch, 2 ch, turn
Rep from Row 2

Relief stitches. A three-dimensional chunky pattern.
Unit of 2 ch
Row 1: miss 1 ch, *1 tr in each ch*, 1 ch, turn
Row 2: *1 dc in each tr*, 2 ch, turn
Row 3: *1 raised htr round front of 1 tr of Row 1, 1 tr in next dc*, 1 ch, turn
Row 4: *1 dc in top of raised htr, 1 dc between raised htr and the tr*, 1 dc in turning ch, 2 ch, turn
Row 5: *1 raised htr round front of raised htr of 2 rows below, 1 tr in next dc*, 1 ch, turn
Rep from Row 4

Steps. Pattern moves on the diagonal.
Unit of 8 ch plus 3
Row 1: miss 2 ch, *1 tr in each ch*, 2 ch, turn
Rows 2 and 3: miss 1 tr, *4 raised tr round front, 4 raised tr round back*, 1 tr in top ch at beg of Row 1, 2 ch, turn
Row 4: miss 1 tr, 1 raised tr round back, *4 raised tr round front, 4 raised tr round back*, 3 raised tr round back, 1 tr in turning ch, 2 ch, turn
Row 5: miss 1 tr, 3 raised tr round front, *4 raised tr round back, 4 raised tr round front*, 4 raised tr round back, 1 raised tr round front, 1 dc in turning ch, 2 ch, turn
Rep from Row 4, moving pattern one st to left on even rows

Crochet stitches

Shells

A **shell** is a group of stitches, usually three or more, worked into one stitch or chain space. Stitches come together in close formation at the base and spread out at the top so that they resemble seashells or fans. The width and depth of a shell depends on the number of stitches that are in it and the size of the space in which these are worked. The shape, too, can be varied. It is symmetrical when all stitches are the same size, asymmetrical when long and short stitches are combined (see far right, opposite page, for the latter).

The shell is a pretty stitch that has a lacy appearance even in a solid pattern.

Made up in medium-weight or heavy yarns, it is suitable and attractive for a blanket. Worked with fine yarns, it is appropriate for shawls, dressy garments and baby clothing. In any yarn type, the shell stitch makes a nice edging because of its curved shape. Examples can be seen on p. 47.

Because of the shell's comparatively elaborate structure, it is best suited to smooth yarns. It also requires more yarn than simpler stitch types (textures, for example), a factor that must be considered in estimating yarn for your own design. Guidelines for making yarn estimates are on p. 39.

Lacy scallops. Small shells worked in narrow chain spaces form a delicate, open pattern; suitable for a baby garment.
Unit of 6 ch plus 4
Row 1: *miss 5 ch, (2 tr, 3 ch, 2 tr) in next ch*, miss 3 ch, 1 tr in last ch, 3 ch, turn
Row 2: *(2 tr, 3 ch, 2 tr) in 3 ch sp*, 1 tr in top of turning ch, 3 ch, turn
Rep from Row 2

Close scallops. A firm stitch that is moderately scalloped.
Unit of 6 ch plus 1
Row 1: miss 3 ch, 2 tr in next ch, miss 2 ch, 1 dc, *miss 2 ch, 4 tr in next ch, miss 2 ch, 1 dc*, 3 ch, turn
Row 2: 2 tr in 1st dc, *1 dc between 2nd and 3rd tr of next 4 tr group, 4 tr in next dc*, 1 dc in 3 ch sp at beginning of row, 3 ch, turn
Rep from Row 2

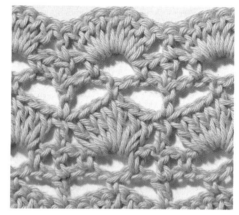

Wide arches. A moderately large pattern in which the shells alternate with open areas.
Unit of 8 ch plus 3
Row 1: miss 2 ch, *1 tr, 3 ch, miss 3 ch, 1 dc, 3 ch, miss 3 ch, *1 tr, 3 ch, turn
Row 2: *1 dc in 2nd ch of 3 ch group, 3 ch, 1 dc in 2nd ch of next 3 ch group, 1 ch, 1 tr in tr, 1 ch*, 1 tr in the turning chain, 3 ch, turn
Row 3: *7 tr in 3 ch sp, 1 tr in tr*, 1 tr in turning chain, 3 ch, turn
Row 4: *3 ch, 1 dc in the centre of the shell, 3 ch, 1 tr in tr*, 1 tr in the turning chain, 3 ch, turn
Rep from Row 2

Simple shells. A moderately large motif.
Unit of 6 ch plus 5
Row 1: miss 3 ch, 1 tr in next ch, *(2 tr, 1 ch, 2 tr) in next ch, yrh, insert hook in next ch, draw up a loop, yrh, draw through 2 loops, miss 3 ch, yrh, insert hook in next ch, draw up a loop, (yrh, draw through 2 loops) 3 times*, 1 tr, 3 ch, turn
Row 2: 1 tr in tr before the ch sp, *(2 tr, 1 ch, 2 tr) in ch sp, yrh, insert hook in next tr, draw up a loop, yrh, draw through 2 loops, miss 3 sts, yrh, insert hook in next tr, draw up a loop, (yrh, draw through 2 loops) 3 times*, work last st in top of turning ch, 3 ch, turn
Rep from Row 2

Arcade stitch. Lacy but firm; the pattern repeats on the diagonal.
Unit of 6 ch plus 8
Row 1: miss 1 ch, 1 dc in each of next 2 ch, *3 ch, miss 3 ch, 1 dc in each of next 3 ch*, 3 ch, miss 3 ch, 1 dc in each of last 2 ch, 1 ch, turn
Row 2: 1 dc in 2nd dc, *5 tr in 3 ch sp, 1 dc in 2nd dc of 3 dc group*, turn
Row 3: *3 ch, 1 dc in each of 3 central tr*, 2 ch, 1 dc in turning chain, 3 ch, turn
Row 4: 2 tr in 2 ch sp, *1 dc in 2nd dc, 5 tr in 3 ch sp*, 1 dc in 2nd dc, 3 tr in 3 ch sp, 1 ch, turn
Row 5: 1 dc in each of first 2 dc, *3 ch, 1 dc in each of 3 central tr*, 3 ch, 1 dc in last tr, 1 dc in turning chain, 1 ch, turn

Wave stitch. A popular pattern for baby blankets and rugs. The crest of each wave is formed with one shell stitch; the distance between the crests can be varied, if you wish, by adjusting the multiple.

Unit of 13 ch

Row 1: miss 3 ch, 4 tr in next 4 ch, 3 tr in next ch, 5 tr in next 5 ch, *miss 2 ch, 5 tr in next 5 ch, 3 tr in next ch, 5 tr in next 5 ch*, 3 ch, turn

Row 2: miss 1 st, 4 tr in next 4 sts, 3 tr in next st, 5 tr in next 5 sts, *miss 2 sts, 5 tr in next 5 sts, 3 tr in next st, 5 tr in next 5 sts*, on the last multiple, end with 4 tr, miss 1 tr, 1 tr in turning ch, 3 ch, turn
Rep from Row 2

Fan stitch. Elegant large shells.

Unit of 14 ch plus 2

Row 1: miss 1 ch, 1 dc, *miss 6 ch, 1 long tr [yrh, insert hook, draw up a loop 1.5 cm long, yrh, draw through 2 loops, yrh, draw through 2 loops], 12 more long tr in the same ch, miss 6 ch, 1 dc*, 3 ch, turn

Row 2: 1 long tr in 1st dc, *5 ch, 1 dc in 7th of 13 long tr, 5 ch, 2 long tr in dc between the fans*, 2 long tr in last dc, 1 ch, turn

Row 3: 1 dc between the 1st 2 long tr, *13 long tr in the dc worked at the centre of fan in previous row, 1 dc between the 2 long tr of previous row*, 3 ch, turn
Rep from Row 2

Starburst. Shells and clusters combined.

Unit of 8 ch plus 10

Row 1: miss 1 ch, 1 dc, *miss 3 ch, 9 tr in next ch, miss 3 ch, 1 dc*, 3 ch, turn

Row 2: miss 1 st, 4 tr cluster over next 4 sts [(yrh, insert hook, draw up a loop, yrh, draw through 2 loops) in each st, yrh, draw through 5 loops], *4 ch, 1 dc, 3 ch, 9 tr cluster over next 9 sts*, 4 ch, 1 dc, 3 ch, 5 tr cluster, 4 ch, turn

Row 3: 4 tr in top of 5 tr cluster, 1 dc in dc, *9 tr in top of 9 tr cluster, 1 dc in dc*, 5 tr in top of 4 tr cluster, 3 ch, turn

Row 4: miss 1 tr, *9 tr cluster, 4 ch, 1 dc, 3 ch*, 1 dc in turning ch, 1 ch, turn

Row 5: 1 dc, *9 tr in top of 9 tr cluster, 1 dc*, 1 dc in turning ch, 3 ch, turn
Rep from Row 2

Bushy stitch. These shells are a combination of double and treble crochet stitches, and are asymmetrical in form.

Unit of 3 ch plus 1

Row 1: miss 3 ch, (1 tr, 2 ch, 1 dc) in next ch, *miss 2 ch, (2 tr, 2 ch, 1 dc) in next ch*, 2 ch, turn

Row 2: *(2 tr, 2 ch, 1 dc) in each 2 ch sp*, 2 ch, turn
Rep from Row 2

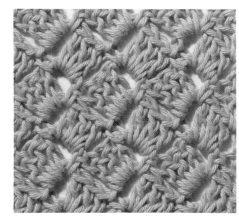

Brick stitch. Squares of asymmetrical shells with openwork between them.

Unit of 4 ch plus 6

Row 1: miss 3 ch, *2 tr in next 2 ch, (1 tr, 3 ch, 1 tr) in next ch, miss 1 ch*, 3 tr in last 3 ch, 3 ch, turn

Row 2: *(3 tr, 3 ch, 1 dc) in each 3 ch sp*, 1 tr between last group of 3 tr and turning ch, 3 ch, turn
Rep from Row 2

Ripple stitch. Asymmetrical shell stitches in a compact pattern; also pretty worked in two or more colours.

Unit of 3 ch plus 1

Row 1: miss 2 ch, 2 tr in next ch, *(1 dc, 2 tr) in next ch, miss 2 ch*, 1 dc, 2 ch, turn

Row 2: 2 tr in 1st dc, *(1 dc, 2 tr) in each dc of previous row*, 1 dc in turning ch, 2 ch, turn
Rep from Row 2

Crochet stitches

Clusters

A **cluster** is a group of three or more stitches worked into one stitch or chain space, then drawn together at the top with one loop. Depending on how many stitches are in the group, results may be relatively flat, as in the soft cluster stitch directly below, or extremely chunky, as in the bobble stitch (lower right). Whatever the type, however, all clusters stand out from a flat surface, thus providing extra texture and dimension in the finished piece.

In an all-over pattern (examples below), the cluster makes a warm, somewhat bulky fabric that is suitable for a heavy sweater or a blanket. Used indi-vidually, or as one row in a plain crochet pattern, it is an attractive accent or trimming. It also works well in patchwork motifs (see pp. 24–25), where it contributes symmetry and textural interest.

Generally, clusters look best in heavy or medium-weight yarn. When estimating the yarn quantity, remember that each cluster is composed of several yarn loops, so half again or even twice as much yarn will be needed as for a simpler stitch, such as a mesh or texture.

In working a cluster, the yarn tension should be kept fairly loose to make the clusters soft, and to facilitate drawing the final loop through the top.

Lace clusters. A bubbly texture of thick puffs combined with openwork.
Unit of 6 ch plus 4
Row 1: miss 3 ch, *(1 tr, 2 ch, 1 tr) in next ch, miss 2 ch, 1 puff [(yrh, insert hook, draw up a loop) 4 times in the same ch, yrh, draw through 9 loops], 1 ch, miss 2 ch*, (1 tr, 2 ch, 1 tr) in last ch, 3 ch, turn
Row 2: *1 puff in 2 ch sp between 2 tr of previous row, 1 ch, (1 tr, 2 ch, 1 tr) under loop that closes the puff in previous row*, 1 puff, 1 tr in 3 ch sp at beg of previous row, 3 ch, turn
Row 3: (1 tr, 2 ch, 1 tr) in top of puff, *1 puff in 2 ch sp, 1 ch, (1 tr, 2 ch, 1 tr) in top of puff*, 1 tr in 3 ch sp at beg of previous row, 3 ch, turn
Rep from Row 2

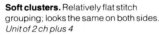

Soft clusters. Relatively flat stitch grouping; looks the same on both sides.
Unit of 2 ch plus 4
Row 1: miss 3 ch, *1 cluster [(yrh, insert hook, draw up a loop, yrn, draw through 2 loops) 3 times in the same ch, yrh, draw through 4 loops], 1 ch, miss 1 ch*, 1 cluster, 3 ch, turn
Row 2: *1 cluster in ch between clusters of previous row*, 1 cluster in top of turning ch, 3 ch, turn
Rep from Row 2

Ball stitch. Soft rounded clusters combined with double crochet.
Unit of 4 ch plus 3
Row 1: miss 1 ch, *1 dc in each ch*, 1 ch, turn
Row 2: 3 dc, *1 ball [(yrh, insert hook, draw up a loop) 3 times in the same st, yrh, draw through 7 loops], 3 dc*, 1 ch, turn
Row 3: *1 dc in each st*, 1 ch, turn
Row 4: 1 dc, *1 ball, 3 dc*, 1 ball, 1 dc, 1 ch, turn
Row 5: *1 dc in each st*, 1 ch, turn
Rep from Row 2

Large clusters. A thicker stitch than soft clusters above, but still fairly flat.
Unit of 2 ch plus 4
Row 1: miss 3 ch, *1 cluster [(yrh, insert hook, draw up a loop, yrh, draw through 2 loops) 4 times in the same ch, yrh, draw through 4 loops, yrh, draw through 2 loops], 1 ch, miss 1 ch*, 1 cluster, 3 ch, turn
Row 2: *1 cluster in each ch sp of previous row, 1 ch*, 1 cluster in top of turning ch, 3 ch, turn
Rep from Row 2

Bobble stitch. Solid, three-dimensional pattern; be sure to allow ample yarn.
Unit of 3 ch plus 1
Row 1: miss 1 ch, *1 dc in each ch*, 1 ch, turn
Row 2: *1 bobble [(yrh, insert hook, draw up a loop, yrh, draw through 2 loops) 5 times in same st, yrh, draw through 6 loops], 2 dc*, 1 bobble, 1 ch, turn
Rows 3 and 5: *1 dc in each st*, 1 ch, turn
Row 4: *2 dc, 1 bobble*, 1 dc, 1 ch, turn
Row 6: 1 dc, *1 bobble, 2 dc*, 1 ch, turn
Rep from Row 2

Motifs

A motif is a self-contained design unit which may be symmetrical or asymmetrical. Motifs can be used singly or joined together in a patchwork.

The centre of a motif is usually a chain joined with a slipstitch to form a ring. The first row, called a *round*, is worked into this circle, with stitches taken over the chain, and adjusted to fit evenly around. Each subsequent round is worked from the right side and closed with a slipstitch at the starting point (unless the form is a spiral). The last round is fastened off.

Motifs can be used individually for appliqué, for example, or as coasters, place mats or potholders. Because there is no limit to their size, you can even fashion a rug. The most popular use for motifs, however, is patchwork. Square patterns, familiarly known as 'granny squares', are frequently used for this, but any symmetrical design will do. Larger items are easy to manage because motifs can be done one at a time, and joined at your leisure. Motifs are also ideal for using up yarn leftovers, as each round can be worked in a different colour (see p. 302 for how to change yarn colours). You can join motifs with an overcast stitch, or crochet them together with slipstitch or double crochet.

Posy. Use this for an appliqué or as the centre portion of a larger motif.
6 ch and join in a ring with ss
Round 1: 2 ch, 23 dc in ring, ss in 2nd ch at beg of rnd to close
Round 2: 4 ch, 1 tr in same st as last ss, 1 ch, (miss 2 st, 1 tr, 2 ch, 1 tr in next st, 1 ch) 7 times, ss in 2nd ch at beg of rnd to close
Round 3: 2 ch, (1 htr, 2 ch, 2 htr) in 2 ch sp at beg of Round 2, 1 dc in 1 ch sp, *(2 htr, 2 ch, 2 htr) in 2 ch sp, 1 dc in the 1 ch sp*, rep from 1st* 6 times, ss in 2nd ch at beg of rnd
Round 4: *(3 tr, 1 ch, 3 tr) in the 2 ch sp, 1 dc on each side of the dc*, rep from 1st* 7 times, ss to 1st tr, fasten off

Clover. The lucky kind with four leaves. For the traditional variety, turn to p. 30.
5 ch and join in a ring with ss
Round 1: 14 dc in ring
Round 2: 2 dc, 1 leaf [4 ch, (yrh twice, insert hook in next st, draw up a loop, yrh, draw through 2 loops, yrh, draw through 2 loops) 3 times in same st, yrh, draw through 4 loops, 3 ch], 1 dc in each of next 2 st, 3 more leaves as above, make stem [6 ch, work back along these 6 ch with 1 dc in each ch (or with a ss in each ch if yarn is thick)], ss in 1st dc to close, fasten off

Daisy. Chain stitches form the petals of this three-dimensional motif.
6 ch and join in a ring with ss
Round 1: 14 dc in ring, ss to 1st dc at beg of rnd to close
Round 2: (into front strand of each dc work 1 dc, 6 ch, 1 dc) 14 times, ss to 1st dc to close
Round 3: (into back strand of each dc work 1 dc, 8 ch, 1 dc) 14 times, ss to 1st dc, fasten off

Star. The conventional five-pointed shape to use as an emblem or decoration.
2 ch
Round 1: 5 dc in 2nd ch from hook
Round 2: 3 dc in each dc
Round 3: (1 dc in next st, 6 ch, ss in 2nd ch from hook, 1 dc in next ch, 1 htr in next ch, 1 tr in next ch, 1 dtr in next ch, 1 dtr in base of starting dc, miss 2 dc) 5 times, ss in first dc to join, fasten off

Chrysanthemum. Broad petals that curl slightly towards the centre.
4 ch and join in a ring with ss
Round 1: 13 dc in ring, ss to 1st dc at beg of rnd to close, fasten off
Round 2: using 2nd colour, work 1 petal into the front strand of each dc of Round 1 [1 dc, 5 ch, 1 dc in 2nd ch from hook, 1 htr in each of next 2 ch, 1 dc in next ch, 1 dc in dc at beg], total of 13 petals
Round 3: work 1 petal into the back strand of each dc of Round 1 [1 ss, 6 ch, 1 dc in 5 of these 6 ch], total of 13 petals, fasten off

Crochet stitches

Motifs/Patchwork

Eyelet square. A simple centre motif surrounded by rows of double crochet; more interesting when worked in two or more colours. Round 1 is crocheted over a double yarn strand instead of the usual ring of chains.
Wind yarn twice around tip of index finger to form a ring
Round 1: 16 dc in ring
Round 2: (1 dc, 10 ch, miss 3 dc) 4 times, ss in 1st dc, fasten off
Round 3: using new colour, (11 dc in the 10 ch sp, 1 dc in next dc) 4 times, ss in 1st dc, fasten off
Round 4: using new colour, *1 dc in each of 6 sts, 2 dc in next st to form corner, 1 dc in each of 5 sts*, rep from *3 times, ss in 1st dc, fasten off
Round 5: 1 dc in each st and 2 dc at each corner, ss in 1st dc
Rep Round 5 as many times as desired for size, changing colours as it suits you, fasten off

Hawaiian square. Large clusters surround a small flower; a very simple motif.
8 ch and join in a ring with ss
Round 1: 1 large cluster in ring [(yrh, insert hook, draw up a loop) 4 times, yrh, draw through 9 loops], (2 ch, 1 large cluster) 7 times, 2 ch, ss in 1st st
Round 2: ss into next 2 ch sp, 1 large cluster in this sp, *2 ch, 1 large cluster in next sp, 2 ch, (1 tr, 2 ch, 1 tr) in next large cluster to form corner, 2 ch, 1 large cluster in next sp*, after tr group at end of rnd, 2 ch, ss into 1st large cluster
Round 3: ss into next 2 ch sp, 1 large cluster in this sp, *(2 ch, 1 large cluster) in each sp up to the corner, 2 ch, (1 tr, 2 ch, 1 tr) between tr groups at corner*, 2 ch, ss in 1st st
Rep from Round 3, working 1 more large cluster on each side for each rnd until there are 6 large clusters on each side, or until the square is the desired size, fasten off

Flower in a square. Long chains are the flower petals.
5 ch and join in a ring with ss
Round 1: 12 dc in ring, ss in 1st dc to close
Round 2: (11 ch, ss in next dc) 12 times
Round 3: ss in each of 1st 6 ch of 1st ch loop, *4 ch, 1 dc, in central st of next ch loop, 4 ch, 1 cluster in next ch loop [(yrh, insert hook, draw up a loop, yrh, draw through 2 loops) 3 times in same ch loop, yrh, draw through 4 loops], 4 ch, 1 cluster in same ch loop to form corner, 4 ch, 1 dc in next loop*, rep from *3 times
Round 4: 2 ss in 1st 4 ch sp, 3 ch, (yrh, insert hook in same sp, draw up a loop, yrh, draw through 2 loops) twice, yrh, draw through 3 loops, *4 ch, 1 dc in next 4 ch sp, 4 ch, (1 cluster, 4 ch, 1 cluster) in corner sp, 4 ch, 1 dc in next 4 ch sp, 4 ch, 1 cluster in next 4 ch sp*, rep from *3 times, 4 ch, ss in top of 1st cluster to close, fasten off

Old America square. This is a traditional type of granny square. It is usually worked in two or more colours.
6 ch and join in a ring with ss
Round 1: 3 ch, 2 tr in ring, 2 ch, (3 tr in ring, 2 ch) 3 times, ss in top of beg ch, fasten off
Round 2: join new colour with ss in 1st ch sp, 3 ch, (2 tr, 2 ch, 3 tr) in same sp to form corner, (1 ch, 3 tr, 2 ch, 3 tr in next 2 ch sp) 3 times for 3 more corners, ss in top of beg ch, fasten off
Round 3: join new colour with ss in 1st 2 ch sp, 3 ch, (2 tr, 2 ch, 3 tr) in the sp, *(1 ch, 3 tr) in each 1 ch sp (along the side), (1 ch, 3 tr, 2 ch, 3 tr) in each 2 ch sp (a corner)*, ss in top of beg ch, fasten off
Rep Round 3 as many times as desired for size

Hexagon. A simple, solid pattern.
6 ch and join in a ring with ss
Round 1: 2 ch, 2 tr in ring, 3 ch, (3 tr in ring, 3 ch) 5 times, ss in top of beg ch to close, fasten off
Round 2: using new colour, 4 ch, *(3 dtr, 2 ch, 3 dtr) in each 3 ch sp*, ss in top of beg ch to close, fasten off
Round 3: using new colour, 3 ch, *1 tr in each dtr, (2 tr, 2 ch, 2 tr) in each 2 ch sp*, ss in top of beg ch to close, fasten off
Round 4: using new colour, 3 ch, *miss 1 st, 1 tr in next st, 1 tr in the missed st*, 1 tr in last st, ss in top of beg ch to close, fasten off

Paddle wheel. The rounds are left open in this hexagonal spiral.
5 ch and join in a ring with ss
Round 1: (6 ch, 1 dc in ring) 6 times, do not close the round
Round 2: (4 ch, 1 dc in next sp) 6 times
Round 3: (4 ch, 1 dc in next sp, 1 dc in next dc) 6 times
Round 4: (4 ch, 1 dc in next sp, 1 dc in each of the 2 dc) 6 times
Round 5: (4 ch, 1 dc in next sp, 1 dc in each of the 3 dc) 6 times
Rep for as many rnds as desired, working 1 extra dc in each group on each rnd; beginning with the 10th rnd, work 5 ch for each sp instead of 4

Dogwood. Four large petals.
2 ch
Round 1: miss 1st ch, 8 dc in 2nd ch, ss in 1st dc to close
Round 2: 5 ch, miss 1 st, 1 dc in next st, (4 ch, miss 1 st, 1 dc in next st) twice, 4 ch, ss in 1st of 5 ch at beg of rnd
Round 3: ss in next ch sp, 3 ch, 6 tr in same sp as ss, (2 ch, 7 tr) in each of next 3 ch sp, 2 ch, ss in top of 4 ch at beg of rnd
Round 4: 2 ch, 1 dc in joining st, (1 dc in each of next 2 st, 2 dc in next st) twice, *(2 dc in next st, 1 dc in each of next 2 st) twice, 2 dc in next st*, rep from * twice, ss in top of beg ch
Round 5: 3 ch, 1 tr in joining st, 1 tr in next st, 2 tr in next st, 1 tr in next st, (2 tr in next st) twice, (1 tr in next st, 2 tr in next st) twice, 2 ch, turn
Round 6: (1 dc, 4 tr, 1 dc, 2 ch, miss 2 sts) twice, ss to bottom of turning ch, fasten off
Rep Rounds 5 and 6 for 3 other petals, each time starting with right side facing you

Wagon wheel. A versatile pattern; besides patchwork, it would be suitable for household items such as table mats or cushion covers.
4 ch and join in a ring with ss
Round 1: 3 ch, 1 petal in ring [(yrh, insert hook, draw up a loop) twice, yrh, draw through 5 loops, 1 ch], 7 more petals in ring, ss in top of beg ch, fasten off
Round 2: join new colour in 1st ch sp, 2 ch, 1 tr in 1st ch sp, 2 ch, (2 tr, 2 ch) in each of next 7 ch sp, ss in 2nd ch at beg, fasten off
Round 3: join new colour in 1st ch sp, 2 ch, (1 tr, 1 ch, 2 tr, 1 ch) in 1st ch sp, (2 tr, 1 ch, 2 tr, 1 ch) in each of next 7 ch sp, ss in 2nd ch at beg, fasten off
Round 4: join new colour in 1st ch sp, 2 ch, 2 tr in 1st ch sp, 1 ch, (3 tr, 1 ch) in each of next 15 ch sp, ss in 2nd ch at beg, fasten off
Rep Round 4 as many times as desired for size, but after Round 5, work 2 ch between tr groups

Crochet stitches

Meshes

A **mesh** consists of chain stitches and treble crochets combined in such a way that they form open spaces. By itself, or in conjunction with other techniques, it has a wide variety of uses.

Either of the square meshes below can serve as the basic element in **filet crochet** (see p. 28). To produce filet, selected meshes are filled with double crochet to form a pattern. (Or sometimes the reverse: the background is filled and open meshes form the pattern.) Once used extensively for doilies and antimacassars, filet is today used more for trimming and accessories. Square meshes also form the back-

ground for **overlaid patterns** (see p 29); in this technique, the spaces are filled with chain stitches, or yarns or ribbons are woven in. Diamond, honeycomb and diamond picot stitches, on the right, are used in the working of **Irish crochet** (see p. 30); as meshes, they form the lace background to flower and leaf motifs.

Used alone, any mesh pattern is ideal for a shawl, providing lightweight warmth. Mesh is also suitable for summer garments, evening wear and baby clothing. For the most lacy effect use lightweight yarns. Good choices are crochet cotton and fine knitting yarn.

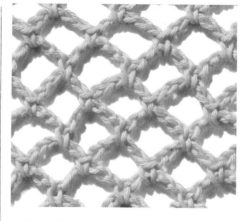

Diamond mesh. A flexible stitch that is especially suitable for a flat round item such as a doily or tablecloth. It is also used in fringe-making and sometimes to join solid sections that have been knitted or crocheted.
Unit of 4 ch plus 2
Row 1: miss 1 ch, 1 dc in next ch, *5 ch, miss 3 ch, 1 dc in next ch*, 1 dc, 5 ch, turn
Row 2: *1 dc in next ch sp, 5 ch*, turn
Rep from Row 2

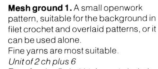

Mesh ground 1. A small openwork pattern, suitable for the background in filet crochet and overlaid patterns, or it can be used alone.
Fine yarns are most suitable.
Unit of 2 ch plus 6
Row 1: miss 5 ch, *1 tr in next ch, 1 ch, miss 1 ch*, 1 tr, 4 ch, turn
Row 2: miss 1st tr of previous row, *1 tr in next tr, 1 ch*, 1 tr in 3rd ch at beg of previous row, 4 ch, turn
Rep from Row 2

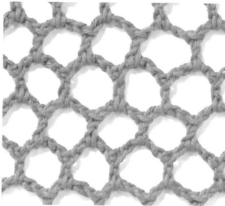

Honeycomb mesh. A popular pattern for backgrounds in Irish crochet (p. 30).
Unit of 4 ch plus 10
Row 1: miss 9 ch, *1 tr in next ch, 4 ch, miss 3 ch*, 1 tr, 8 ch, turn
Row 2: *1 tr in the 4 ch sp, 4 ch*, 1 tr, 8 ch, turn
Rep from Row 2

Mesh ground 2. An openwork pattern with larger spaces than the one above; can be worked with heavier yarns. Two treble crochet stitches are needed to fill a space, if this is used for filet crochet.
Unit of 3 ch plus 8
Row 1: miss 7 ch, *1 tr in next ch, 2 ch, miss 2 tr*, 1 tr, 5 ch, turn
Row 2: miss 1st tr of previous row, *1 tr in next tr, 2 ch, miss 2 tr*, 1 tr in 3rd ch at beg of previous row, 5 ch, turn
Rep from Row 2

Diamond picot mesh. Another favourite pattern for Irish crochet; this one has been used as a background for the cushion cover shown on p. 31.
Unit of 7 ch plus 2
Row 1: miss 1 ch, 1 dc in next ch, *2 ch, 1 picot [5 ch, ss in 1st of these 5 ch], 3 ch, 1 picot, 2 ch, miss 6 ch, 1 dc*, 2 ch, turn
Row 2: 1 picot, 3 ch, 1 picot, 2 ch, 1 dc in ch sp between picots of previous row, *2 ch, 1 picot, 3 ch, 1 picot, 2 ch, 1 dc in ch sp*, 2 ch, turn
Rep from Row 2

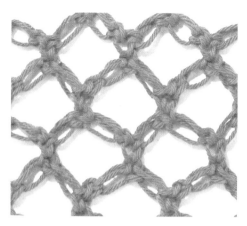

Solomon's knot. Lengthened chains form an open mesh that is similar in appearance to netting. The lengthened loop can be adjusted as desired. See p. 13 for the way to make the knots.
Unit of 4 ch plus 2
Row 1: miss 1 ch, 1 dc, 1 single knot [lengthen loop on hook to 1.5 cm, draw up a loop, take hook across front of lengthened loop and insert it under yarn of ch just completed, work 1 dc], make another single knot to complete the double knot, *miss 3 ch, 1 dc in next ch, 1 double knot*, 1 single knot, turn (total of 3 single knots for turning)
Row 2: *1 dc in centre of double knot in previous row, 1 double knot*, 1 single knot, turn
Rep from Row 2

Trestle stitch. A lacy pattern with alternating large and small spaces. Suitable for a shawl.
Unit of 4 ch plus 6
Row 1: miss 5 ch, *1 tr in next ch, 3 ch, miss 3 ch*, 1 tr, 4 ch, turn
Row 2: *1 dc in 2nd ch of 3 ch group, 2 ch, 1 tr in next tr, 2 ch*, 1 dc in turning ch of previous row, 5 ch, turn
Row 3: *1 tr in the tr, 3 ch*, 1 tr in turning ch of previous row, 4 ch, turn
Rep from Row 2

Open chequers. A large mesh ground with the alternate spaces filled in.
Unit of 6 ch plus 3
Row 1: miss 3 ch, 1 tr in each of next 2 ch, *3 ch, miss 3 ch, 1 tr in each of next 3 ch*, 3 ch, miss 3 ch, 1 tr in last ch, 3 ch, turn
Row 2: 2 tr in 1st ch sp, *3 ch, 3 tr in next 3 ch sp*, 3 ch, 1 tr in top of turning ch, 3 ch, turn
Rep from Row 2

Shaping mesh ground

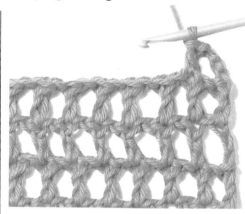

To decrease a space at the end of a row, do not work the last space (the one formed by the turning chain); instead, work 4 ch (for mesh ground 1) or 5 ch (for mesh ground 2) and turn; work 1 treble crochet in the next treble crochet. The resulting space will be triangular rather than square.

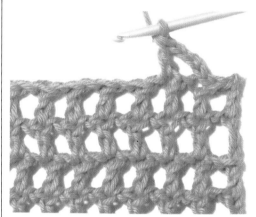

To decrease a space at the beginning of a row, do not work the usual turning chain; instead work 1 ch and turn; work 1 slipstitch in each chain stitch up to the next treble crochet, then 1 slipstitch in the treble crochet; work 4 ch (for mesh ground 1) or 5 ch (for mesh ground 2) and continue with the mesh pattern starting with 1 treble crochet in the next stitch. Use this method only when decreases must be paired on either side of the work.

To increase a space at the beginning of a row, do not work the usual turning chain; instead, work 5 ch (for mesh ground 1) or 7 ch (for mesh ground 2) and turn; work 1 treble crochet in the first stitch of the previous row.

Crochet stitches

Filet crochet

Filet crochet is a square mesh pattern with certain spaces filled to form a motif. Appropriate stitches for the openwork are mesh grounds 1 and 2 on p. 26. The filling is treble crochet, one stitch for a small space, two for a large one. Directions are usually charted, with background meshes represented by blank squares and motif stitches by filled ones. To follow a chart, read from right to left on the odd (right side) rows, from left to right on the even rows. Do the reverse, if you are left-handed. Suitable filet motifs are monograms, geometric shapes and flowers. Cotton is the traditional choice of thread.

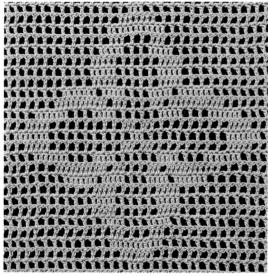

Flower motif. Suitable for an insertion or an all-over repeat.

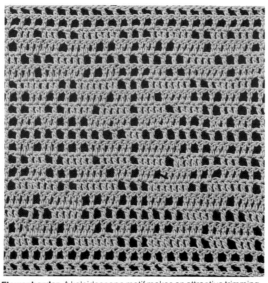

Flower border. A kaleidoscope motif makes an attractive trimming.

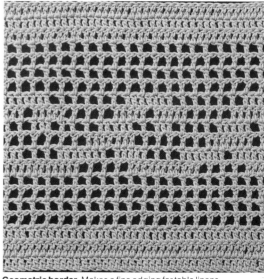

Geometric border. Makes a fine edging for table linens.

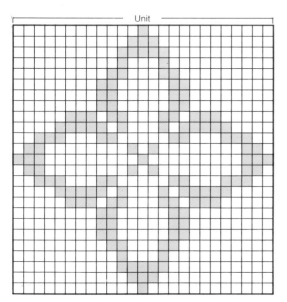

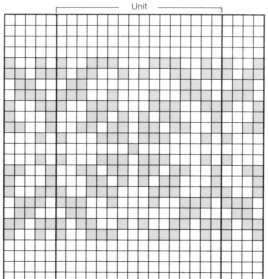

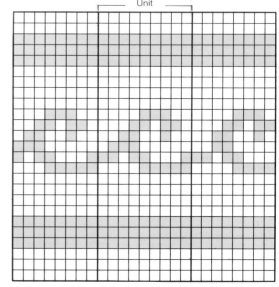

Overlaid meshes

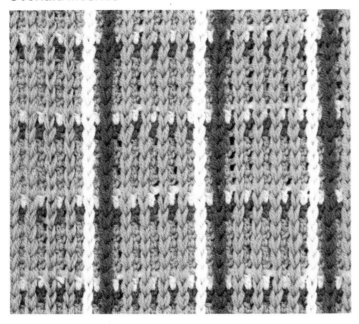

Chained overlay. A mesh background with chain stitches worked in the spaces. An easy and effective way to create a crocheted stripe or plaid. Depending on the weight and type of yarn you choose, this technique can be used for a garment, a place mat, a cushion cover or a rug. The colour sequences should be planned before you begin.

To prepare the background,
use pattern for mesh ground I (p. 26).
To work the overlay chains,
use 2 strands of yarn; make a slip knot. With right side of mesh facing you, and yarn held behind the work, draw a loop through the first space in the lower right corner, insert hook in space directly above it, draw a loop through the space and the loop on the hook. Continue working this way to the top of the mesh, then begin again at bottom. In forming the chains, take care to maintain an even tension, or the background may be distorted.

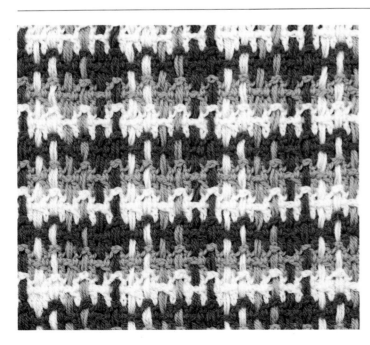

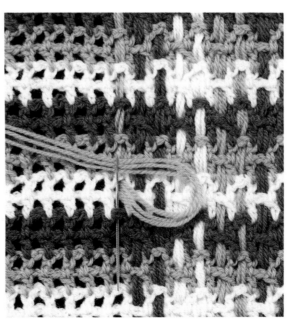

Woven overlay. Yarns intertwined with a mesh background. The fabric produced is thick and firm, usable for outerwear, a place mat or rug. Though any stitch might be used, a mesh (shown here) is the usual choice. The woven strands can be yarn, fabric strips or ribbon, and can be worked into the background vertically, horizontally or diagonally.

To prepare the background,
use pattern for mesh ground I (p.26).
To weave the overlay,
use 3 strands of yarn threaded in a tapestry (blunt-ended) needle. Lace the yarns vertically under and over the chain bars, filling alternate spaces on each row. Yarn should be pulled firmly so that no loops remain, yet not too tightly, or the mesh may pucker.

Crochet stitches

Irish crochet

Irish crochet was developed in the mid-19th century, its style inspired by a popular Venetian lace. The lovely designs are most elegant worked in fine cotton or linen yarns. A typical pattern consists of floral motifs set in a mesh background. The mesh is usually worked around motifs, but in some modern adaptations it is crocheted separately and the motifs applied to it. A three-dimensional look can be given to the motifs by working certain portions over an additional yarn strand called a foundation cord. This cord, which is used also to control shaping, should be about twice the thickness of the working yarn.

Shamrock. Wind foundation cord twice around index finger and slip it off.
Round 1: 2 dc in ring, 1 picot [4 ch] (10 dc in ring, 4 ch) twice, 8 dc in ring, ss to 1st dc, pull cord so sts lie flat
Round 2: 15 dc over cord only, miss 1 picot and 1 dc; over cord and sts make 1 dc in each of next 7 dc, pull cord so sts lie flat, 18 dc over cord only, miss 1 picot and 1 dc, 1 dc in each of next 7 dc, 15 dc on cord only, miss 1 picot and 1 dc, 1 dc in each of next 7 dc
Round 3: drop cord, round 1st leaf (1 ch, 1 dc) in each of next 2 sts, (1 ch, 1 tr) in each of next 3 sts, (1 ch, 1 dtr) in each of next 5 sts, (1 ch, 1 tr) in each of next 3 sts, (1 ch, 1 dc) in each of next 2 sts, ss in dc between leaves, work other 2 leaves as the 1st, but work 7 dtr in 2nd leaf, ss between leaves
Round 4: pick up foundation cord, miss 1st ch, *3 dc in each of next 2 ch, 4 ch*, rep from * round leaf, omitting last 4 ch, pull up cord, continue same way round other 2 leaves, ss to close
Short stem: 30 dc over cord, 1 ch, turn, leave loop of cord at end, work back up stem with 1 dc in each dc, ss to base
Long stem: same as short one but 160 dc

Loop for adjusting stem

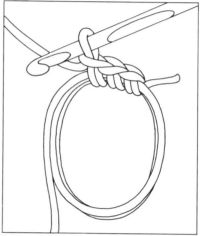

To form motif centre, wind foundation cord over index finger 1, 2, or 3 times (if number is not in directions, determine it by cord thickness). Slip ring off and work centre stitches over it. When ring is complete, pull cord gently to bring stitches close together. Work subsequent rounds over the cord where indicated in directions (stitches are

made over cord alone or over both cord and stitches). As work progresses, pull cord gently to keep stitches close together.
When motif is complete, cut the cord and working yarn, leaving ends at least 15 cm long. Using a rug or tapestry needle, weave each yarn end into the motif back for about 1.5 cm. Cut ends off.

Leaf. Worked over foundation cord and stitches, pulling up the cord periodically to make stitches lie flat. 15 ch, lay foundation cord over ch.
Row 1: miss 1 ch, *1 dc in each ch*, 5 dc in last ch (to form the tip), 1 dc in each loop along opposite side of ch, 3 dc over foundation cord only (to go around base), 1 dc in back loop of each dc on 1st side of ch, ending 4 dc from the centre dc in leaf tip, 1 ch, turn
Row 2: picking up front loop only, 1 dc in each dc down side, 3 dc in centre dc at base, 1 dc in each dc up other side, ending 3 dc from tip, 1 ch, turn
Row 3: picking up back loop, 1 dc in each dc down side, 3 dc in centre dc at base, 1 dc in each dc up other side, end 3 dc from tip of previous row, 1 ch, turn
Rows 4 and 6: as Row 3, working front loop only **Row 5:** as Row 3, working back loop only. Fasten off at end of Row 6

Rose. 8 ch and join in a ring with ss
Round 1: 6 ch, (1 tr, 3 ch) 7 times, ss in 3rd ch at beg or rnd
Round 2: (1 dc, 1 htr, 3 tr, 1 htr, 1 dc) over each 3 ch loop
Round 3: working behind Round 2, work 1 ss in ss of Round 1, 5 ch, (1 ss in next tr of Round 1, 5 ch) 7 times, ss in 1st ss to close
Round 4: (1 dc, 1htr, 5 tr, 1 htr, 1 dc) over each 5 ch loop
Round 5: working behind Round 4, work 1 ss in 1st ss of Round 3, 7 ch, (1 ss in next ss of Round 3, 7 ch) 7 times, ss in 1st ss to close
Round 6: (1dc, 1 htr, 7tr, 1 htr, 1 dc) over each 7 ch loop
Round 7: working behind Round 6, work 1 ss in 1st ss of Round 5, 9 ch, (1 ss in next ss of Round 5, 9 ch) 7 times, ss in 1st ss to close
Round 8: (1 dc, 1 htr, 9 tr, 1 htr, 1 dc) over each 9 ch loop, fasten off

Irish crochet cushion top

This lovely cushion is a fine way to display your talent for crochet. Approximate sizes are given, but the best result will be obtained if you crochet the top first, and then make or buy a cushion to fit.

Materials

200 g of No. 8 and 100 g No. 5 crochet cotton (for foundation cord); steel crochet hook 1.75 mm to obtain mesh tension; tapestry needle; 38 cm square of light-coloured muslin to work on; tacking thread and needle, 1 cushion of about 30 or 34 cm square, covered with plain, smooth fabric

Tension

For mesh, 16 chains to 5 cm

For motifs, no tension can be specified, but approximate sizes are: leaf, 5.5 cm from tip to base; shamrock, 5.5 cm from top to stem; rose 6.5 cm in diameter

Preparing the grid. Draw a 30 cm square on muslin. Mark off 2.5 cm segments along each side, then use the marks to draw lines diagonally (see illustration below). Work mesh over this.

Making motifs. Following the instructions on the opposite page, make one rose, eight leaves, two shamrocks with short stems facing in opposite directions, two shamrocks with long stems facing in opposite directions (to reverse a stem, turn it over just before slipstitching it to the base). Finish off all of the foundation cords except the ones extending from the long shamrock stems. Assemble the motifs and attach them to the grid as directed below.

Making the mesh. Work Rows 1 and 2, then tack the mesh to the grid, right side up, and follow instructions below.

98 ch and check your tension

Row 1 (wrong side): miss 1 ch, 1 dc, *2 ch, 1 picot [5 ch, ss in 1st of these 5 ch], 3 ch, 1 picot, 2 ch, miss 7 ch, 1 dc in next ch*, turn

Row 2: 10 ch, 1 picot, 2 ch, 1 dc in the 3 ch sp between picots of previous row, *2 ch, 1 picot, 3 ch, 1 picot, 2 ch, 1 dc in the 3 ch sp*, turn

Row 3: 2 ch, 1 picot, 3 ch, 1 picot, 3 ch, 1 picot, 2 ch, 1 dc in 3 ch sp, *2 ch, 1 picot, 3 ch, 1 picot, 2 ch, 1 dc in the 3 ch sp*, work last dc in the 10 ch sp of the previous row, turn

Repeat Rows 2 and 3 for pattern.

After mesh is attached to grid, each right-side row is worked with the grid facing you right-side up; for a wrong-side row, grid must be turned upside-down and the mesh pulled away from it slightly. Wherever mesh comes in contact with a motif, slipstitch it to one edge of the motif, then chain enough stitches to move up a row or to continue horizontally on the wrong side of the motif.

When mesh is complete, connect diamonds along top and left edges with *8 ch, 1 dc in each 3 ch sp*

Forming a border. Cut a length of foundation cord 152 cm long. Starting at one corner, work (5 dc, 5 ch) 3 times over cord and each 8 ch group. Pull up cord periodically to make stitches lie flat. Do not fasten off foundation cord until after cover has been mounted, as some adjustment may be necessary.

Finishing. Detach crocheted piece carefully from grid; remove tacking threads. Pin it to one side of cushion, adjusting fit either by stretching gently or pulling on the foundation cord. Sew the border with double thread, taking small stitches through back of border and under cushion fabric; weave foundation cord into back of border for 3 cm; cut remainder. Tack rose to prevent shifting. Steam-press lightly.

To assemble motifs, lay them out in the arrangement shown. Join seven leaves first, making small stitches at contact points. Next, attach rose and bottom leaf. Join shamrocks where picots touch, then draw up cords on stems, shaping them as shown. Sew each stem in position, cut its cord, weave end into the back. Centre motifs on grid; tack their centres to fabric, leaving edges free.

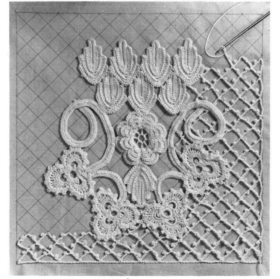

To crochet mesh around motifs, work first 2 rows, then tack foundation chain to bottom line of grid with the 10-ch group at right edge, mesh lines aligning with grid lines. Work 3rd row of mesh, taking it behind shamrocks as necessary. Continue up right side to top of motifs; fasten off; work left side, then top, tacking mesh to grid as work proceeds. Complete border as directed above.

Sew the completed piece by hand to one side of cushion, centring it between finished edges, as shown, or attaching it along the seams (if it fits precisely). Smooth fabric, in a dark or medium colour, sets off this lace to best advantage. For laundering, it would be wise to remove lace to avoid the risk of the colour running. Wash it gently by hand, wet-block on grid; re-sew to cushion when dry.

Crochet stitches

Tunisian crochet

Tunisian crochet (also called afghan stitch) is a cross between knitting and crochet methods. The fabric is similar to a knitted one, but firmer, especially suited to blankets, coats or suits.

To work these stitches, you need a special tool called a *tricot needle* or *hook*. This is longer than other types, uniform in diameter, and has a knob at one end to keep stitches from sliding off. The procedure is to work from right to left on one row, leaving all loops on the hook, then from left to right on the next row, never turning the work.

The foundation of most afghan stitches is two basic rows (see below); the finish can be one row of either slip-stitch or double crochet. Blocking is essential and must be done carefully, as this fabric tends to pull on the bias.

BASIC TECHNIQUE

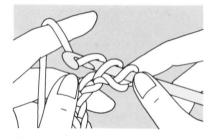

Work the desired number of ch plus 1.
Row 1: miss 1 ch, *insert hook in the next ch, draw up a loop and leave it on the hook*, do not turn work at the end of the row.

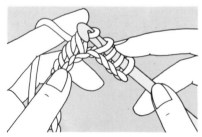

Row 2: yrh, draw yarn through 1st loop on hook, *yrh, draw through 2 loops*, do not turn work; 1 remaining loop counts as 1st st on next row.

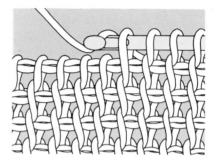

Basic Tunisian (knit stitch). The first two rows of this pattern are used for the foundation of most Tunisian stitches. Its texture, which resembles that of a woven fabric, is especially suitable for cross stitch embroidery.
Unit of any number of ch plus 1
Row 1: miss 1 ch, *insert hook in next ch, draw up a loop*
Row 2: yrh, draw through 1 loop, *yrh, draw through 2 loops*
Row 3: *insert hook right to left under next vertical stitch, draw up a loop*
Rep from Row 2

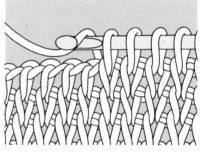

Tunisian stocking stitch. This pattern looks like the knitted version, except that it is thicker.
Unit of any number of ch plus 1
Rows 1 and 2: basic Tunisian
Row 3: *insert hook front to back in the centre of next vertical st loop (the centre can be seen more easily if you separate the 2 yarns using thumb and 3rd finger of left hand), draw up a loop*
Row 4: yrh, draw through 1 loop, *yrh, draw through 2 loops*
Rep from Row 3

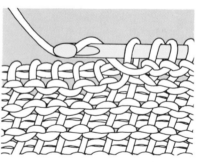

Tunisian purl. Yarn is held in front of work as for purl stitch in knitting.
Unit of any number of ch plus 1
Rows 1 and 2: basic Tunisian
Row 3: *holding yarn to the front, insert hook right to left under next vertical st, draw up a loop*
Row 4: yrh, draw through 1 loop, *yrh, draw through 2 loops*
Rep from Row 3

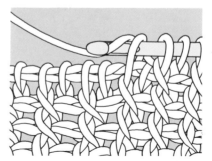

Tunisian crossed stitch. Pairs of stitches are worked in reverse order.
Unit of 2 ch plus 1
Rows 1 and 2: basic Tunisian
Row 3: *miss 1 vertical st, insert hook right to left under next vertical st, draw up a loop, insert hook right to left under missed vertical st, draw up a loop*
Row 4: yrh, draw through 1 loop, *yrh, draw through 2 loops*
Rep from Row 3

Tunisian double stitch. Rows of diagonal stitches alternate with rows of the basic vertical pattern.
Unit of any number of ch plus 1
Rows 1 and 2: basic Tunisian
Row 3: *insert hook right to left under next vertical st, draw up a loop, yrh, draw through 1 loop*
Row 4: yrh, draw through 1 loop, *yrh, draw through 2 loops*
Rep from Row 3

Tunisian popcorn. The knobs are worked on a ground of basic Tunisian. If desired, popcorn size can be increased by lengthening the chain; also, spacing can be varied by adjusting the number of stitches between popcorns.
Unit of 4 ch plus 5
Rows 1 and 2: basic Tunisian
Row 3: draw a loop through each of next 4 vertical sts, *3 ch, draw a loop through each of next 4 vertical sts*
Rows 4, 5, 6: basic Tunisian
Row 7: draw a loop through each side of next 2 vertical sts, *3 ch, draw a loop through each of next 4 vertical sts*, 3 ch, draw a loop through each of next 2 vertical sts.
Rows 8, 9, 10: basic Tunisian
Rep from Row 3

Tunisian rib. A combination of basic and purled Tunisian stitches.
Unit of 6 ch plus 4
Rows 1 and 2: basic Tunisian
Row 3: *3 sts basic Tunisian, 3 sts Tunisian purl*, 3 sts basic Tunisian
Row 4: yrh, draw through 1 loop, *yrh, draw through 2 loops*
Rep from Row 3

Tunisian honeycomb. Knit and purl stitches are alternated in the same way as for knitted moss stitch.
Unit of 2 ch plus 1
Rows 1 and 2: basic Tunisian
Row 3: *1 Tunisian purl under next vertical bar, 1 basic Tunisian under next vertical bar*
Rows 4 and 6: yrh, draw through 1 loop, *yrh, draw through 2 loops*
Row 5: *1 basic Tunisian under next vertical bar, 1 Tunisian purl under next vertical bar*
Rep from Row 3

Tunisian bias stitch. Worked in the same manner as Tunisian crossed stitch (opposite page), but pattern is moved one stitch to the left on alternate rows.
Unit of 2 ch plus 1
Rows 1 and 2: basic Tunisian
Rows 3 and 4: Tunisian crossed stitch
Row 5: draw a loop under next vertical stitch, *cross next pair of stitches*, draw a loop under last vertical stitch
Row 6: yrh, draw through 1 loop, *yrh, draw through 2 loops*
Rep from Row 3

Tunisian lace. An exceptionally pretty pattern that is very easy to work.
Unit of 4 ch plus 1
Row 1: basic Tunisian
Row 2: *3 ch, yrh, draw through 5 loops, yrh, draw through 1 loop*
Row 3: *draw up a loop through the top of each cluster, draw up a loop in each ch of the 3 ch group*
Rep from Row 2

Crochet stitches

Loops

Lattice loop. An airy pattern of elongated loops, especially suitable for a shawl, or one row might be used for a lacy insertion. See below for the way to work a lattice.

Unit of any number of ch

Row 1: miss 1 ch, *1 dc in each dc*, 1 ch, turn

Row 2: lengthen turning ch to height of strip, place strip between the loop and the yarn, draw a loop through the lengthened chain, *insert hook in next st, draw up a loop to top of strip, yrh, draw through the long loop, yrh, draw through 2 loops*, 1 ch, turn

Row 3: *1 dc in each st*
Rep from Row 2

Bouclé loop. Shaggy loops on one side of fabric, double crochet on reverse side. Loops can be worked in two different ways (see below). This stitch is suitable for a cushion cover, rug or garment; bouclé loop can also be knitted.

Unit of any number of ch

Row 1: miss 1 ch, *1 dc in each ch*, 1 ch, turn

Row 2: *1 loop st in each dc*, 1 ch, turn

Row 3: *1 dc in each st*, 1 ch, turn
Rep from Row 2

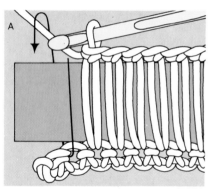

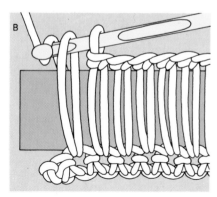

WORKING THE LATTICE LOOP

A lattice can be worked neatly over a ruler or a cardboard strip. If you do not have a ruler in a suitable size, cut a strip of sturdy card about 15 cm long and the desired depth of the stitch.

To begin lattice pattern, work a row of double crochet, 1 chain and turn. Lengthen the turning chain to the height of the strip, place strip between loop and yarn, draw a loop through the lengthened chain, *slide hook forward and down, and insert it in the next stitch, lower yarn behind the strip until it reaches the hook, draw up a long loop (hooking action is indicated by arrow, illustration A), yarn round hook (B), draw a loop through long loop, yarn round hook, draw through remaining 2 loops*. Repeat from asterisk across the row, removing strip and moving it forward as it becomes filled with stitches, 1 chain, turn.

To continue pattern, work a double crochet in each stitch, and on the last stitch, insert hook under the last long loop as well as the two top loops, 1 chain and turn. Repeat the lattice row next or, if preferred, work additional rows of double crochet, then a lattice.

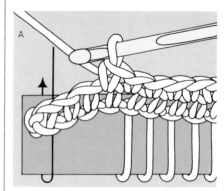

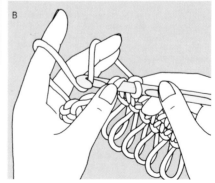

WORKING THE BOUCLÉ LOOP

A bouclé loop can be formed with the aid of an object such as a pencil, ruler or cardboard strip, or it can be worked over one or two fingers of the left hand. The first method is more precise; the second is faster once a rhythm is developed. Before you begin, work a sample to determine the length of the loops. Somewhere between 1 cm and 4 cm is usual. Once established, the loop length should be consistent throughout the pattern.

To form loops over a strip, first work a foundation row of double crochet, 1 chain and turn. *Bracing strip behind the work with left hand, insert hook in next stitch, transfer strip to right hand and take yarn round strip front to back (see arrow, illustration A), draw up a loop, yarn round hook, draw through 2 loops*. Repeat from asterisk to end of row, sliding loops off and moving strip forward as it becomes filled.

To form loops over the fingers, first make a foundation row of double crochet, 1 chain and turn. *Insert hook in next stitch, swing 3rd and 4th fingers on left hand forward under yarn then back against yarn so that a loop is formed over these fingers (B), draw a loop through the stitch, pulling it over top of 3rd finger, yarn round hook, draw through 2 loops, slip fingers out of the loop*. Repeat from asterisk across the row.

Chain loop stitch. Curly loops are worked on a background of double crochet. Different effects can be obtained by making longer chains, or by working the ground in treble crochet. This pattern has the same uses as bouclé loop (left).

Unit of any number of ch plus 2

Rows 1 and 2: double crochet

Row 3: working into front loop of each st *1 dc, 8 ch*, 1 dc, 1 ch, turn

Row 4: *1 dc, working into other loop of each st worked in previous row*, 1 ch, turn
Rep from Row 1

Broomstick lace. A soft and spongy texture; a useful stitch for shawls and baby blankets. The pattern is a combination of large loops, worked over a 'stick' (dowel or large knitting needle), and double crochet, worked over a group of 5 loops.

Unit of 5 ch

Row 1: transfer ch on hook to the stick, * insert hook in next ch, draw up a loop and place it on the stick*, do not turn

Row 2: *insert hook through 5 loops and slide them from stick, draw a loop through the 5 loops, yrh, draw through 1 loop, 4 dc over same 5 loops*, do not turn

Row 3: transfer ch on hook to the stick, *draw up a loop through next dc, place loop on stick*, do not turn
Rep from Row 2

WORKING THE CHAIN LOOP

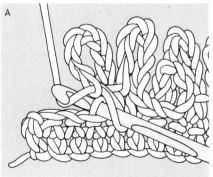

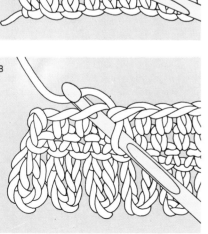

A chain loop is produced by making a long chain between 2 stitches. The crowding of these loops forces them to curl and form a thick, spongy texture on the fabric face.

To begin a chain loop pattern, work 2 rows of double crochet, 1 chain and turn. *Inserting hook into front loop of each stitch (A), work 1 double crochet, 8 chain*. Repeat from *, ending the row with 1 double crochet, 1 chain, turn.

To continue pattern, *insert hook into other loop of each stitch in the previous row (B), work 1 double crochet*, 1 chain, turn.

WORKING BROOMSTICK LACE

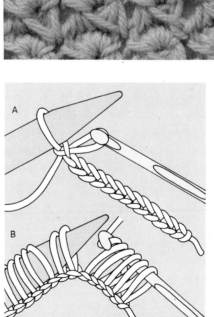

Broomstick loops are formed over a dowel or thick knitting needle, of a diameter between 1 cm and 2.5 cm, and of sufficient length to hold all stitches. To make a blanket, for example, a dowel 2.5 cm thick and 90 cm long might be used. If using a dowel, layers of tape or a few rubber bands should be wrapped round one end to keep stitches from sliding off.

To begin broomstick pattern, work a row of chain divisible by 5, counting the chain on hook. Transfer chain on hook to stick and brace the stick under your left arm. *Insert hook in next chain, draw up a loop (A) and place it on the stick*. Repeat from asterisk across the row; do not turn.

To continue pattern, *insert hook right to left through 5 loops, draw a loop through the 5 loops (B), yarn round hook, draw a loop through the 1 loop, 4 double crochet over the same 5 loops (C)*. Repeat from asterisk across the row; do not turn. All loops are worked from left to right, double crochet rows from right to left (the reverse if you are left-handed).

Crochet stitches/Multicolour

Introduction

Attractive effects are possible with the use of two or more colours in crochet. Because stitches are tall, however, results can never be as subtle or finely detailed as in multicoloured knitting. As a rule, simple designs, such as geometric shapes and stripes, work the best, and double crochet permits the greatest flexibility, with frequent colour changes.

There are three ways of working coloured patterns (also called jacquards), shown on the facing page. Each is suited to a particular situation. A colour change is always made the same way, whichever technique you use. Pick up the new colour as the final yarn round hook in the last stitch of the previous colour (second illustration on right).

WORKING WITH A COLOUR CHART

A chart is often used to give directions for colour patterns in crochet. This is a graph in which each square equals a stitch and each line equals a row. Usually, blank squares represent the main colour, symbols or coloured squares depict the contrasts and, where needed, an accompanying key interprets these usages. To follow a chart, start at the bottom and read from right to left for right-side rows, from left to right for wrong-side rows. It is possible to work crochet from other needlework charts, such as a cross stitch pattern, but a test sample must be made to decide if the proportions translate attractively, and the colour changes are workable.

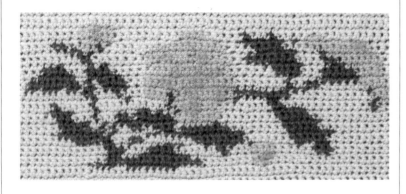

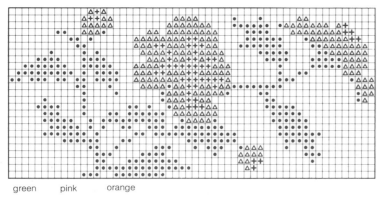

green   pink   orange

Jacquard techniques

To join in a new colour mid-row, lay the yarn end over the row below, introducing it a few stitches before you need it (A). Continue to work with the 1st colour, covering the end of the new yarn. Work the 1st colour to the final 2 loops of the last stitch, then draw the new colour through these last 2 loops (B).

The same technique can be used when changing colours at the beginning of a row by introducing the new colour on the last few stitches of the row below. Joining yarn by this method eliminates the need to weave in the yarn ends with a tapestry needle when the project is complete.

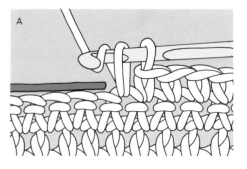

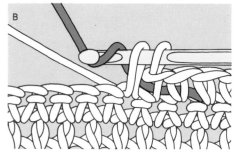

If unused yarn must be carried over more than 3 stitches, it is best to catch it into the work every other stitch. The yarn strands will be less likely to pull or be snagged, and tension will be more even. When using this technique, take care not to apply tension to the yarn being carried, as this will cause the work to pucker.

On a right-side row, insert hook into the stitch, then under the carried yarn at back of the work, catch working yarn with the hook (A), draw up a loop and complete the stitch.

On a wrong-side row, insert hook under the carried yarn, then into the stitch, catch working yarn with the hook (B), draw up a loop and complete the stitch.

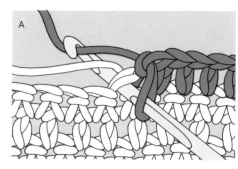

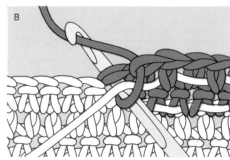

Carrying unused colours across the wrong side is suitable for any crocheted fabric that reveals just one finished surface – a pullover or a cushion cover, for example. If carried over more than 3 stitches, unused yarn should be caught into the work every other stitch (see lower right, opposite page).

To change colours on a right-side row, work the 1st colour to the final 2 loops of the last stitch, drop 1st colour back and to the left of 2nd colour, yrh and draw through 2 loops with 2nd colour.

To change colours on a wrong-side row, work 1st colour to the final 2 loops of the last stitch, drop 1st colour forward and to the right of 2nd colour, yrh and draw through 2 loops with 2nd colour.

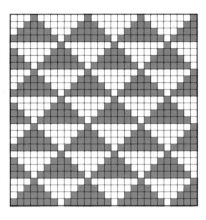  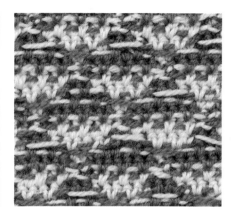

Working over colours not in use is one way to crochet a reversible fabric. This method is faster than cutting and weaving (below), but it consumes more yarn and produces a fabric that is quite heavy. The carried yarn, though covered by the stitches, *is* visible between stitches, and the fabric is attractive or not depending on the design and colours you are working with. Use a hook one size larger than usual to allow for the bulk of the unused yarn.

To carry the unused colour, lay it on top of the previous row as you work stitches in the contrasting colour.

To change colours, draw a loop of the 2nd colour through the final 2 loops of the last stitch in the 1st colour.

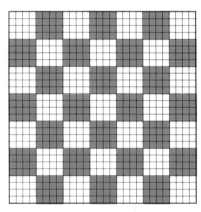  

Cutting and weaving the yarn ends is another way to manage colour changes on a reversible fabric. An alternative to working over yarn (above), this is a practical approach when unused yarn must be carried a great distance, when colours are changed at the end of a row, or when the pattern is an inset motif, as in the example on the right.

To discontinue a colour, work it to the final 2 loops of the last stitch, then draw up a loop with the new colour. Cut off the 1st colour, leaving a 15 cm end. When the work is complete, weave the yarn end through 4 to 6 stitches of the colour that matches it; cut off the remainder.

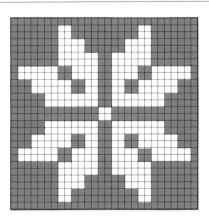  

Crochet stitches/Charted

Shorthand symbols

Crochet techniques can be represented by symbols and the symbols used to chart a pattern stitch, or an entire project, visually. Because a chart resembles the actual look of a pattern, it aids in visualising an unfamiliar stitch. It is especially suited to working in the round.

Listed on the right are symbols, their meanings and the numbers of pages on which illustrations of the techniques can be found. As a rule, no more than a few symbols are used in one pattern, so it is necessary to remember only the ones for which you have immediate use.

Though crochet symbols are used in many countries, they are not standardised. The ones given here are typical, but not universal, examples. If you need a symbol that is not shown here, you can invent your own.

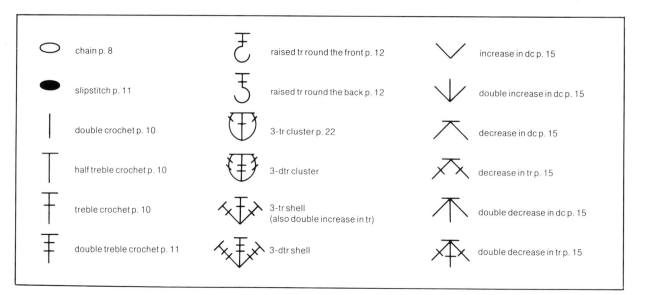

⬭	chain p. 8
⬬	slipstitch p. 11
│	double crochet p. 10
┬	half treble crochet p. 10
╪	treble crochet p. 10
╪	double treble crochet p. 11
	raised tr round the front p. 12
	raised tr round the back p. 12
	3-tr cluster p. 22
	3-dtr cluster
	3-tr shell (also double increase in tr)
	3-dtr shell
∨	increase in dc p. 15
↓	double increase in dc p. 15
⋏	decrease in dc p. 15
	decrease in tr p. 15
⋀	double decrease in dc p. 15
	double decrease in tr p. 15

Charted stitch

Clusters in a square. Directions below, charted form on the right.
6 ch and join in a ring with ss
Round 1: 3 ch, (yrh, insert hook in ring, draw up a loop, yrh, draw through 2 loops) twice, yrh, draw through 3 loops, 2 ch, *3 tr cluster in ring [(yrh, insert hook, draw up a loop, yrh, draw through 2 loops) 3 times, yrh, draw through 4 loops], 2 ch*, rep from *6 more times, ss in top of beg ch
Round 2: 3 ch, 2 tr in 2 ch sp, at end of Round 1 (in front of 3 ch) 2 ch, (3 tr in next 2 ch sp, 2 ch) 7 times, ss in top of beg ch
Round 3: 1 ch, *1 dc in 2nd tr, 2 ch, 3 dtr cluster in next 2 ch sp [(yrh twice, insert hook, draw up a loop, yrh, draw through 2 loops, yrh, draw through 2 loops) 3 times, yrh, draw through 4 loops], rep from *7 more times, ss in beg ch
Round 4: 1 ch, *3 dc in st at top of cluster, (3 tr, 2 ch, 3 tr) in next dc, 3 dc in top of next cluster, 1 ch, 1 dc in next dc, 1 ch*, rep from *5 more times, ss in beg ch
Round 5: 1 ch, 1 dc in each st or ch, 3 dc in each 2 ch sp at corners, ss in beg ch, fasten off

Crocheting a garment

Introduction
Designing a crocheted garment
Charting a woman's cardigan
How to make a garment chart
Shaping necklines
Shaping armholes and sleeves
Ribbing
Buttons
Buttonholes

Introduction

This section contains the basic information necessary to help you understand how crochet patterns are constructed, and to help you plan and design crocheted garments. Before crocheting any garment, read through the instructions to make sure you understand them, and try out any new techniques.

Designing a crocheted garment

There are two ways to design a crocheted garment. One is to alter an existing pattern – making changes to fit your measurements – the other is to design your own. With either method you will need the following:

1. An accurate set of body or garment measurements.

2. A sample square to decide which tension to use to calculate the amount of yarn needed.

3. Squared paper for the pattern.

Before you begin, read pp. 42–43 for information about shaping necklines, armholes and sleeves.

The first thing to do is write down the width and the length measurements for each section of the garment you are planning. If your plan is based on body measurements, you must add ease, around the chest and upper arm for example, using other patterns for guides. You should also add 5 mm for seams, and plan the overall length, for example, from the underarm to the bottom edge of a sweater. Next, choose a yarn and stitch pattern, crochet a sample, or several if necessary, until you are satisfied with the appearance of the stitch, then measure the tension. To translate garment width dimensions into stitches, multiply the stitch tension by centimetres. For example, if you are planning a sweater that measures 45 cm at the bottom edge of the back, and the stitch tension is 8 stitches to 5 cm, you would need (45 ÷ 5 × 8 = 72) 72 stitches plus 2 stitches for seams for the back section. To translate garment length measurements into rows, multiply row tension by centimetres. If a sweater measures 40 cm from bottom edge to underarm, and row tension is 6 rows to 5 cm, there would be (40 ÷ 5 × 6 = 48) 48 rows from bottom to underarm. To determine the number and placing of decreases for shaping armholes, sleeves and neckline, follow the guidelines on pp. 42–43. Prepare a chart or outline (see pp. 40–41 for the method), then calculate the quantity of yarn.

To estimate how much yarn you will need for your own design, there are several approaches; these are described below. One general rule to keep in mind is that pattern stitches with clusters, shells or bobbles usually require about 50 per cent more yarn than the basic stitches and textures (see p. 18).

One way to estimate yarn quantity is to use the amount specified for a similar pattern using similar yarn and stitch. (For this purpose, it is useful to keep a notebook of patterns.) This quantity may not be precisely what you need, so it is advisable to buy extra yarn to be sure of having enough from the same dye lot. Many shops will let you return unused yarn within a reasonable time; check with the shop at the time of purchase.

Another approach is to consult the sales assistant in a wool shop. The assistants usually have the experience from which to make an estimate.

If you cannot find either assistance or an appropriate pattern, here is a way to make your own estimate. Buy a ball of desired yarn and wind off a length of yarn that equals about one-eighth of the total length. Measure this length carefully. It might be, for example, 18 m. Make a tension sample and measure its area; if the sample is 10 cm by 7.5 cm, the area would be 75 sq. cm.

Next, calculate the approximate area for each garment section by multiplying widest measurement by overall length. Add these figures together, then divide the sum by the sample area and multiply this number by the length of yarn used for the sample.

The following is an example:

Sweater

across the chest	45 cm
length, neck to bottom	50 cm
total area	2,250 sq. cm

Sweater front

area, same as back	2,250 sq. cm

Sweater sleeves

width at upper arm	30 cm
overall length	57.5 cm
total area, both sleeves	3,450 sq. cm

Total area for sweater 7,950 sq. cm

Sweater area divided by sample area (75) 106

106 is the approximate number of 10 cm by 7.5 cm samples needed to crochet the garment. Multiply 18 m (length of yarn used in sample) by 106 to determine total amount of yarn – 1,908 m. Deduct 10 per cent for shaping decreases – total of 1,717 m. Divide this by 144 (18 × 8) to get an estimate of balls required (12).

Introduction

Compare the measurements of the pattern with those of the person for whom the garment is intended. When taking body measurements remember that ease must be added to ensure a good fit. If the measurements are not given in the pattern, you can work them out by dividing the total of the row of stitches by the tension width (5cm) and multiplying the answer by the number of stitches in the tension width. For example, if the shoulder has 20 stitches, and the tension is 8 stitches to 5 cm, you divide 20 by 8 which equals 2.5, and multiply this by 5. The answer is 12.5 cm and this is the shoulder measurement.

Crocheting a garment

Charting a woman's cardigan

This tailored cardigan is shown in both written and charted form so you can compare the methods. Directions are for Misses' size 12 (86 cm bust).

Materials

400 g of double knitting yarn, sizes 3.50 and 4.00 hooks, 6 1.5 cm buttons

Tension

8 htr and 6 rows = 5 cm with 4.00 hook

BACK. Using 4.00 hook, 73 ch.

Row 1: miss 1 ch, *1 dc in each ch*, 1 ch, turn (you now have 72 sts).

Row 2: *1 htr in each dc*, 2 ch, turn.

Row 3: *1 htr in each htr*, 2 ch, turn.

Rep Row 3 until piece measures 36 cm.

Armholes: 1 ss in each of 1st 4 sts, 1 htr in each st to last 4 sts, 2 ch, turn; dec 1 st at each end of next 4 rows. Work straight on 56 sts until the armholes measure 20 cm.

Shoulders: 8 ss in 1st 8 sts, 9 htr in next 9 sts, 2 ch, turn; dec 1 st at beg of next row, 1 htr in each of next 6 sts, 1 dc in next st, fasten off. Miss centre 22 sts, join yarn and work other shoulder to match.

LEFT FRONT. With 4.00 hook, 37 ch. **Row 1:** miss 1 ch, *1 dc in each ch*, 1 ch, turn (you now have 36 sts).

Row 2: *1 htr in each dc*, 2 ch, turn.

Row 3: 1 htr in each of 1st 14 htr, 4 raised tr round the front of next 4 dc in Row 1, 1 htr in each of next 18 htr, 2 ch, turn.

Row 4: *1 htr in each htr*, 2 ch, turn.

Row 5: 1 htr in each of 1st 14 htr, 4 raised tr round front of 4 raised tr 2 rows below, 18 htr in next 18 htr, 2 ch, turn.

Repeat Rows 4 and 5 until piece measures 36 cm, ending on wrong side.

Armhole: 1 ss in each of 1st 4 sts, work to end of row; dec 1 st at armhole edge 4 times. Work straight on rem 28 sts until armhole measures 10 cm, ending at front edge.

Shaping neck: 1 ss in each of 1st 8 sts, work to end; dec 1 st at neck edge 4 times. Work straight on rem 16 sts until armhole measures 20 cm, ending at armhole.

Shoulder: 1 ss in each of 1st 8 sts; work to end of row, fasten off.

RIGHT FRONT. Work as for left front reversing the pattern and shapings.

SLEEVES. With 4.00 hook, 33 ch.

Work **Row 1** in dc and **Row 2** in htr as for left front, but on 32 sts.

Row 3: 1 htr in each of 1st 14 sts, 4 raised tr round the front of next 4 dc in Row 1, 1 htr in each of next 14 sts.

Continue in pattern, increasing 1 st at each end on every 4th row, 8 times. Work straight on 48 sts until piece measures 40 cm.

Shaping cap: ss in each of 1st 4 sts, work to last 4 sts, turn; work 1 row, dec 1 st at each end of next and every other row 6 times; dec 1 st at each end of every row 5 times, 18 sts remain, fasten off.

FINISHING. Sew side, shoulder and sleeve seams. With right side facing you, using 3.50 hook, begin at right side seam, work 2 rows of dc along bottom, front and neck edges of sweater; work 3 dc in each corner st. Mark 6 buttonhole positions on right front, placing 1st one

A woman's tailored cardigan is worked in htr with a panel of 4 raised tr on each front and sleeve.

1 cm from neck, last one 1.5 cm from bottom; space others between.

Next round, work in dc, making a horizontal 1 ch buttonhole at each marking and 3 dc at each corner. Work 2 more rounds of dc, decreasing round curve of neck; fasten off. With right side facing you, using 3.50 hook, work 5 rnds of dc along bottom of each sleeve. Sew in sleeves. Attach buttons.

How to make a garment chart

A garment chart is a visual representation of written instructions. There are two different forms – **outline** and **graph**. Either can be used when designing a garment or adjusting an existing pattern.

An outline is a drawing of the exact dimensions of each main garment section, with shaping information written on it. This form gives you a realistic view of garment shape, and can be used later, if desired, for blocking. To make an outline, use sturdy wrapping paper and start by drawing a straight line on it equal to the widest dimension (usually the underarm) of the garment back,

then draw a second line perpendicular to and through the centre of the first. Using these as reference points, measure the other areas. Draw the sleeve and any other garment sections in the same way.

A graph is worked out on paper marked off in squares. Each square represents a stitch, each line of squares a

row. To chart this way, the tension must already have been determined. You can graph an entire garment section, or just those areas that are shaped (as shown opposite); only half need really be graphed. A graph is a less realistic view of garment shape than an outline, but it is easier to follow.

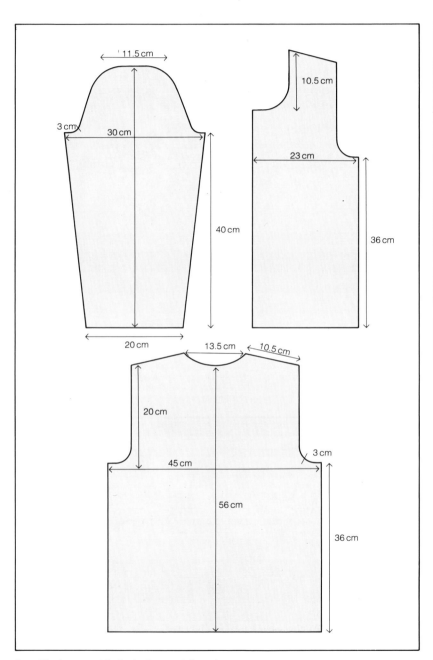

An outline is an exact duplicate of garment dimensions.

1/2 sleeve

24 stitches

48 rows

16 stitches

1/2 back

11 stitches

24 rows

36 stitches

Front

8 stitches

24 rows

36 stitches

In a graph, each square represents a stitch, each line of squares a row.

Crocheting a garment

Shaping necklines

Special care should be taken in crocheting a neckline; this part of a garment is particularly noticeable. In general, the fit should be smooth, with no gaping or wrinkling. In the case of a high neck on a pullover, a slit opening must be provided so that the head can pass through. (There is not enough stretch in crochet for the neckline to expand.)

The neck width calculation is based on shoulder width and equals about one-third of it, or the number of stitches that remain after subtracting the two shoulder lengths. Front neck depth is calculated in relation to armhole depth, and varies according to style (see the directions on the right). Usually, a back neck is straight, formed by leaving the stitches unworked just below the last row of shoulder shaping. If a front is a deep scoop or square, the back may be shaped the same way, but would be less deep as a general rule.

In shaping a neckline, work is usually divided, each half crocheted separately, and all decreases made on the right side of the work. Distribution of decreases depends to some extent on stitch height. You can miss one or two rows between decreases for a short stitch (dc or htr), but should decrease every row for a tall one (tr and taller), or the edge will be jagged.

A crocheted neck edge may be naturally neat – a square neck is an example – but it will hold its shape better and have a more finished appearance if you work an edging. One or more rows of double crochet makes a firm edge. Ribbing is also suitable. It can be crocheted (see p. 44) or knitted by picking up stitches along the edge. Shoulder seams should be joined before the edging is added.

Guidelines for making three basic neck shapings are shown on the right. These are typical, but do not represent all possibilities. If you wish to use them for altering an existing pattern, or designing your own, chart the design first.

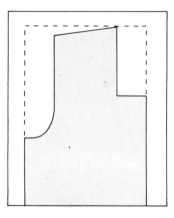

Square neckline shaping is begun 8 cm to 15 cm below the start of shoulder shaping by leaving unworked all stitches allotted for the neckline opening. (The number of stitches for the neck is what remains after subtracting stitches for each shoulder.) There is no decreasing for this style; you work straight up to the shoulder, completing one-half of the neckline at a time.
To make the edging shown here, work 2 rounds of double crochet along the neck edge, starting and ending at one shoulder seam, decreasing 1 stitch at each corner.

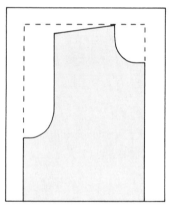

High round neckline shaping is begun about 5 cm below shoulder for an adult garment, 4 cm for a child's. One-third of stitches to be decreased are left unworked at the centre; another third are allotted to each half of the neck, decreasing at the neck edge 1 stitch every row, then working even to the top of the shoulder.
A slit opening must be provided for this style; usually it is worked at the back by dividing the work at the centre, 8 cm to 10 cm below the shoulder.
To make the edging shown here, work 3 rows of double crochet, starting and ending at the slit, decreasing where necessary (usually in the curved areas) to keep the edging flat.

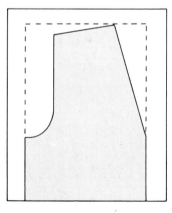

A V-neckline is usually started 15 cm to 23 cm below the shoulder, or just after the start of armhole shaping. Work is divided at the centre and each half is worked separately, decreasing gradually at the neck edge, always on the right side of the work. For a wide V, decrease 1 stitch every row; for a narrower one, every second or third row. If you have an odd number of stitches across the front, decrease centre stitch before dividing work.
To make the edging shown here, work 1 round of double crochet on the neck edge, then a second round of reverse double crochet, starting and ending at a shoulder seam, decreasing 2 stitches at the V on each round.

Shaping armholes and sleeves

Armhole and sleeve shapings are important to crocheting a well-fitted garment. Three basic styles are described below – **classic, raglan** and **semi-raglan.**

To chart an armhole with the methods given here, you need measurements for *shoulder width,* the *chest* (or underarm) across half the garment, plus the standard *shoulder length* and *armhole depth* for your garment size and *neck circumference* (for raglan only). To shape a sleeve, you should have the *wrist,* the *underarm*

length and the *upper-arm* measurements.

The usual way of crocheting a sleeve is from the bottom edge up, increasing the underarm seam gradually and symmetrically between the wrist and the underarm. The armhole and sleeve cap are

shaped with decreases. To avoid a jagged decrease underarm, follow the instructions on p. 16 for decreasing several stitches at the beginning and end of a row. These methods are appropriate also for shaping the shoulder seam.

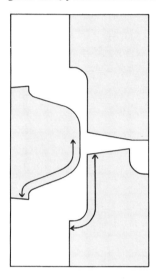

A classic armhole shape is formed by subtracting the stitches needed for shoulder width from the number at the underarm. Half this figure is the number of stitches to decrease for each armhole. At start of shaping, decrease at least 3 cm of stitches, then decrease remainder over next few rows. Work even until correct depth is reached.
For set-in sleeve cap, decrease the same number of stitches as at beginning of armhole. Continue decreasing symmetrically until cap length is the same as armhole length; work 1 more row and fasten off.

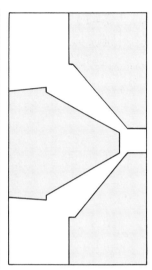

A raglan armhole ends at the neckline and must be planned in relation to it. It is shown here combined with a square neckline, a simple combination often used in crocheted garments. To determine the number of decreases, subtract the stitches for neck width from the number of stitches at the underarm. Start raglan with 1.5 cm of decreases on each side; distribute remaining decreases symmetrically and evenly over the number of rows needed to reach the neckline.
Shape top of sleeves the same way, having 8 cm to 15 cm at neck edge depending on neckline depth.

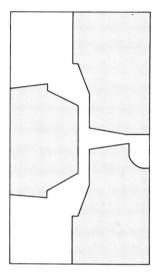

A semi-raglan armhole is shaped like a raglan on the lower half, like a classic armhole on the upper half and shoulder. Calculate the number of decreases as for a classic armhole, but instead of distributing them over the first 4 to 5 rows, space them in a sloped line over half the armhole depth; work evenly for the remaining depth.
For the sleeve cap, decrease symmetrically over the same number of rows as for the armhole; work 1 more row straight across and fasten off.

A set-in sleeve has a symmetrically curved cap.

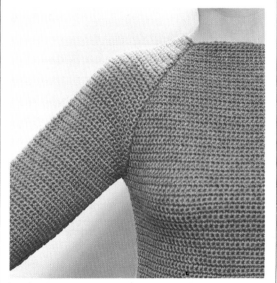

A raglan sleeve is shaped in a continuous slope to neckline.

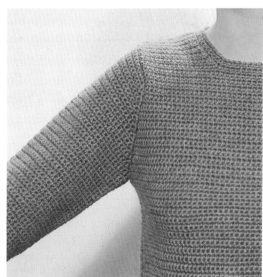

A semi-raglan sleeve has raglan slope combined with a wide cap.

Crocheting a garment

Ribbing

Crocheted ribbing is used on the edges of a garment to provide a firm and somewhat elastic finish. Four variations are described below. The easiest of the four to produce is the ridge stitch, in which the ribs are worked horizontally, then turned and the garment pattern worked along one side edge to obtain the vertical effect. All the other rib patterns are worked vertically.

Crocheted ribbing is not as elastic as knitted ribbing and never fits as snugly. You can, if you prefer, knit the ribbed edging for a crocheted garment. The usual method is to work the garment, join the seams, then pick up stitches along the edge. As a general rule, one knitted stitch is picked up for each crocheted one. Make a sample to decide correct needle size.

Ridge stitch ribbing. Ridges are formed horizontally, then turned sideways for ribbing.
Unit of any number of ch that will form desired depth of ribbing
Row 1: miss 1 ch, *1 dc in each ch*, 1 ch, turn
Row 2: *1 dc in back loop of each st*, 1 ch, turn.
Repeat Row 2 for the pattern. When ribbing is long enough for the garment edge on which it is to be used, fasten off yarn; sew the ends together, then work the pattern stitches along one side of the ridge pattern.

Raised stitch ribbing 1. Vertical ridges are formed on two sides.
Unit of 2 ch plus 1
Row 1: miss 1 ch, *1 dc in each ch*, 1 ch, turn
Row 2: *1 raised dc round the front, 1 raised dc round the back*, 1 dc in last sp, 1 ch, turn
Row 3: *1 raised dc round the front, 1 dc under the 2 crossed strands of next raised st*, 1 dc in last sp, 1 ch, turn
Repeat Row 3 for pattern

Raised stitch ribbing 2. Vertical ridges are on one side only.
Unit of 2 ch
Row 1: miss 1 ch, *1 dc in each ch*, 1 ch, turn
Row 2: 1 dc, *1 raised tr round the front of next stitch, 1 dc in next st*, 1 ch, turn
Row 3: *1 dc in each st*, 1 ch, turn
Row 4: 1 dc, *1 raised tr round front of raised st 2 rows below, 1 dc in next st*, 1 ch, turn
Repeat Rows 3 and 4 for pattern

Tunisian crochet ribbing. Ridges are less pronounced than in other crocheted ribbings, but this is a neat pattern, particularly suited to a garment of Tunisian crochet.
Unit of 2 ch
Rows 1 and 2: basic Tunisian
Row 3: 1 Tunisian purl under 2nd bar, *1 Tunisian stocking st, 1 Tunisian purl*
Row 4: yrh, draw through 1 loop, *yrh, draw through 2 loops*
Repeat Rows 3 and 4 for pattern

Buttons

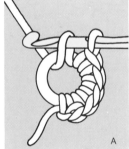

Ring button. Yarn is worked over a plastic ring 3 mm smaller than button size. To start, make a slip knot. Inserting hook through ring to form each st, work round it in dc (A) until ring is completely covered; ss in 1st st to close, fasten off. Cut yarn leaving 30 cm; thread the end in tapestry needle. Oversew a st in each outside loop (B), then pull stitches towards centre. Tie beginning and end strands together, then sew an X across the button back for attaching it to the garment.

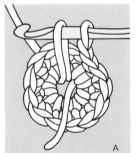

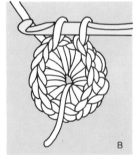

Ball button. Yarn is worked into a three-dimensional motif; size and thickness depend on yarn weight. 3 ch and join in ring with ss. **Round 1:** 1 ch, 8 dc in ring, ss to beg ch. **Round 2:** 1 ch, (1 dc in next st, 2 dc in next st) 4 times, ss to beg ch; pull the short yarn end up through centre hole. **Round 3:** 1 ch, (insert hook through centre hole, draw up a long loop (A), yrh, draw through 2 loops) 16 times, ss to beg ch. **Round 4:** 1 dc in every other st, fasten off; oversew and finish back as for ring button.

Buttonholes

Horizontal buttonhole, double crochet.

At the beginning of buttonhole position, work a number of chain stitches that will accommodate the diameter of the button (usually from 1 to 5). Miss the number of stitches for which you have chains, then continue in pattern (A).
Next row. Work over the buttonhole chain in double crochet, making the same number of stitches as there are chains (B).

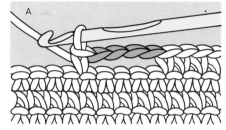

A 4-chain buttonhole completed

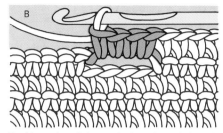

Double crochet stitches worked over buttonhole chain

Horizontal buttonhole, treble crochet.

Insert hook under diagonal strand halfway down last stitch (A), *draw up a loop, yarn round hook, draw through 2 loops, insert hook under left strand at front of last stitch*, repeat from * to * for desired length. To complete buttonhole, draw up loop, miss same number of stitches as made for buttonhole, insert hook in next stitch, draw up a loop, complete a treble crochet (B).

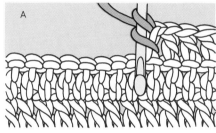

Inserting hook under the diagonal yarn

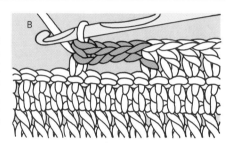

A double-chain buttonhole completed

Vertical buttonhole, any stitch.

On right side of garment, work across the row to buttonhole position; turn and continue to work this half until depth of buttonhole has been obtained. If the number of buttonhole rows is uneven, fasten off yarn (A), weave into back of work later; if even, leave yarn at side of work. Starting at buttonhole edge, attach yarn, work second half to match the first. Next row, start at side edge and continue in pattern across both sections (B).

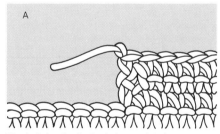

First half of vertical buttonhole completed

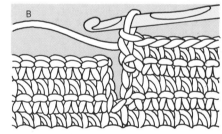

Second half of vertical buttonhole completed

Buttonhole loop of double crochet.

On a right-side row, work to end of buttonhole position. Work a chain the same length as buttonhole, join it to beginning of buttonhole thus: slip hook out of chain, insert it front to back through top of stitch, hook chain and pull it through; insert hook in next stitch to the right, yarn round hook (A), draw a loop through both stitch and chain. Work double crochet over chain, slipstitch in stitch where chain was started (B); continue in pattern.

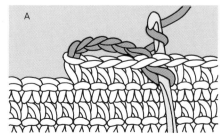

Joining chain to beginning of buttonhole

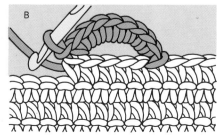

Working double crochet over buttonhole loop

Assembling and finishing

General information
Joining sections right sides together
Joining sections edge to edge
Crocheted edgings and insertions

General information

There are several ways to finish crochet; select methods that suit your needs and work patiently for professional results.

Blocking is generally the first step. This procedure shapes crocheted pieces to specific measurements and, at the same time, usually smooths slight stitch irregularities. There are two basic blocking methods – steam (for wool and other natural yarns), and wet (for highly textured stitches). Before beginning, check the yarn label; some yarns should not be blocked.

Joining is the step after blocking for any project worked in sections. There are several methods (see below). Selection should be made according to, first, the needs of the situation, then personal preference. Joining with a seam allowance (right sides together) is necessary when edges are uneven; it is often preferred for its firm and neat appearance. Joining edge to edge is possible only when edges are even and have the same number of stitches. This method is especially suitable for ribbings and motifs.

Edging may be applied as a final step to provide extra firmness and a uniform appearance for a crocheted edge. Suggestions for finishes are given opposite.

JOINING SECTIONS RIGHT SIDES TOGETHER

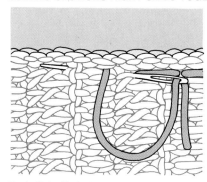

Backstitch. Worked any distance from edge; use for uneven edges or to alter garment.
Bring needle up through 2 corresponding stitches; *insert through 2 stitches behind thread (where thread emerges for last stitch); bring up through 2 stitches in front of the thread.*

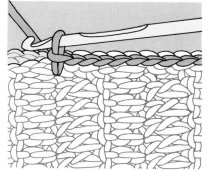

Slipstitch. A firm joining that is suitable for seams in which minimal stretch is required.
Draw up a loop through a corresponding stitch on each section; *insert hook through the next 2 stitches; draw a loop through both stitches and the loop on the hook.*

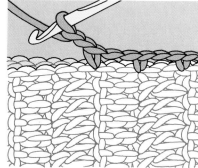

Slipstitch plus chain. A more flexible joining than plain slipstitch; use for bulky yarns or when a greater degree of stretch is desired.
Work slipstitch through 2 corresponding stitches at start of row; *make a chain equal to height of row; work slipstitch at point of next row.*

JOINING SECTIONS EDGE TO EDGE

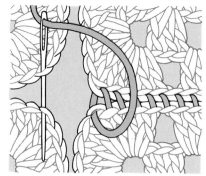

Overcasting. Used mainly to join patchwork motifs. ***Insert needle** at a right-angle under back loop of a corresponding stitch on each edge; draw yarn through.* When you reach the corners of 2 motifs, continue as shown above.

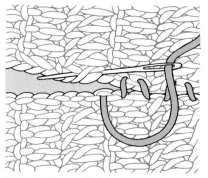

Mattress stitch. An invisible joining, especially suited to taller stitches and filet.
Lay sections right side up. *Take needle under lower half of edge stitch on one piece, then under upper half of edge stitch on adjacent piece.*

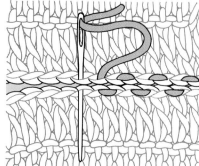

Weaving top or bottom edges. Invisible joining for straight edges with equal numbers of stitches.
Right sides up, *bring needle up through 1 loop, down through next loop on one edge; weave down and up through 2 loops on other edge.*

Crocheted edgings and insertions

Crochet lends itself so naturally to use as a trimming that pattern possibilities are nearly endless. Worked along the edge of crochet or knitting (see directly below), it serves to make an edge firm, give it a neat look, and reinforce its shape with a distinctive outline. When applied to a garment, seams should be joined first and the edge stitch begun at one seam. Worked separately, a trimming can be crocheted horizontally (examples in centre row) or vertically (bottom row), and sewn to crocheted, knitted or woven fabrics. Any yarn is suitable so long as it is compatible with the fabric to which it is applied.

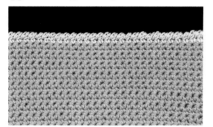

Double crochet edging. Use one to four rows for sleeveless armholes or a neckline, at least 2 to 3 cm for front or bottom edges of a garment.

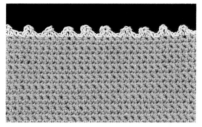

Corded edging. A very firm and neat trimming.
Row 1: double crochet, worked right to left
Row 2: slipstitch, worked left to right

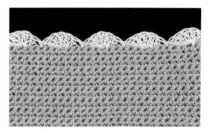

Little picot edging. For a child's dress.
Every row: *1 ss in each of next 2 sts, 1 dc in next st, 3 ch, 1 dc in same st as last dc*

Scalloped edging. Suitable for any lacy item.
Every row: 1 ss, *miss 2 sts, 5 tr in next st, miss 2 sts, 1 ss in next st*

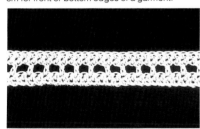

Eyelet insertion. Unit of 2 ch plus 2
Row 1: miss 1 ch, *1 dc in each ch*, 1 ch, turn
Row 2: *1 dc in each dc*, 4 ch, turn
Row 3: miss 2 dc, *1 tr in next dc, 1 ch, miss 1 dc*, 1 tr in last dc, 1 ch, turn
Row 4: *1 dc in each tr, 1 dc in each ch*, 1 ch, turn
Row 5: *1 dc in each dc*, fasten off

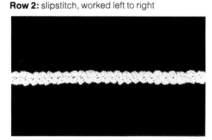

Twisted braid. Unit of any number of ch
Row 1: miss 1 ch, *insert hook in next ch, draw up a loop, twist hook horizontally and clockwise 1 full turn, yrh, draw through 2 loops*; at end of row, 1 ch and continue round opposite side of ch; repeat instructions between asterisks in each loop on that side; fasten off

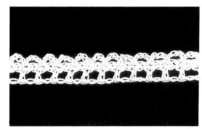

Filet and picot edging. Unit of 2 ch plus 4
Row 1: miss 5 ch, 1 tr in next st, *1 ch, miss 1 ch, 1 tr in next st*, 1 ch, turn
Row 2: 1 dc in each st and ch sp, 4 ch, turn
Row 3: miss 1 dc, *ss in next dc, 4 ch, miss 1 dc*, ss in 4th ch at beg of Row 1, fasten off

Fancy scalloped edging. Unit of 5 ch plus 3
Row 1: miss 1 ch, *1 dc in each ch*, turn
Row 2: ss in 1st dc, *3 ch, miss 3 dc, ss in next 2 dc*, turn
Row 3: ss in 1st 2 ss, *(1 tr, 1 ch) 4 times in next 3 ch sp, 1 tr in same sp, 2 ss*, turn
Row 4: *(1 dc, 3 ch in next 1 ch sp) 4 times, ss in next 2 ss*, fasten off

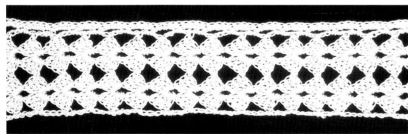

Double shell edging. 19 ch. **Row 1:** miss 9 ch, 1 shell [4 tr, 3 ch, 4 tr] in next ch, miss 5 ch, 1 shell in next ch, miss 2 ch, 1 trtr in last ch, 5 ch, turn. **Row 2:** 1 shell in each ch sp of shell below, 1 trtr in last tr of 2nd shell, 5 ch, turn. Repeat Row 2 for pattern, ending last row with 2 ch, 1 tr in last tr; do not turn. **Along one edge,** 1 ch, 1 dc in loop just formed, *3 ch, 1 dc in next loop* for entire length, 1 ch, turn. **Next row:** 1 dc in 1st dc, *3 dc in next 3 ch sp, 1 dc in next dc*, fasten off.

Looped edging. 13 ch. **Row 1:** miss 6 ch, 1 dtr in next ch, 9 ch, miss 5 ch, ss in last ch, 1 ch, turn. **Row 2:** in 9 ch sp (3 dc, 3 ch) 5 times, 2 dc in same sp, 1 dc in dtr, 2 dc in 6 ch sp, 5 ch, turn. **Row 3:** miss 2 dc, 1 dtr in next dc, 9 ch, miss 2 3 ch loops, ss in next 3 ch loop, 1 ch, turn. **Row 4:** in 9 ch sp (3 dc, 3 ch) 5 times, 2 dc in same sp, 1 dc in dtr, 1 dc in 4th ch of turning ch, 5 ch, turn. Repeat Rows 3 and 4 for desired length; fasten off.

Blanket in Tunisian crochet

This wool blanket, approximately 122 cm by 160 cm, is worked in Tunisian crochet.

Twenty-five geometric blocks form the basis of this blanket. Each block is worked in the basic Tunisian stitch, bordered with double crochet, then embroidered with cross stitch to create the centre motif.

Materials

Double knitting wool, 900 g of beige, 800 g of blue, 6 mm tricot needle or hook, rug needle, knitting bobbins (optional)

Tension

8 sts and 7 rows = 5 cm

Preparation

Make several butterflies of each colour wool, allowing 5 to 6 m of yarn for each one.

MAKING A BLOCK. With blue, 34 ch

Rows 1–6. Work in basic Tunisian stitch, and at the end of each row insert hook under both the last bar and the yarn directly behind it. This makes a firm edge on which to work the border.

Row 7. Pick up 3 loops in blue and then *change colours* as follows. Make a slip knot 10 cm from the end of the beige yarn; pull up this loop through the next stitch, leaving short yarn end at back to be woven in later. Pick up 27 more beige loops; fasten in a new blue yarn with a slip knot; pick up 3 blue loops.

Row 8. Work off 2 loops in blue, then pick up beige yarn from under the blue, thus *twisting* the yarns; draw it through the last blue loop and 1 beige loop. Continue with beige until 1 beige loop remains; pick up blue yarn from under the beige; work off last 4 loops in blue. Continue in pattern, adding new colours where needed (you will have 7 butterflies on Row 27), and twisting yarns when changing colours on the return rows. When the square is finished, do not fasten off, but continue with blue.

Border. Across the top work 2 dc under the 2nd bar, *1 dc under the next bar*, 2 dc in the last bar. Continue down the left side with 1 dc under the double loop of each bar; continue along bottom with 2 dc in the first ch, *1 dc in the next ch*, 2 dc in the last ch; work up the right side with 1 dc under both loops of each end st; join with a ss to the 1st dc; fasten off. Weave all yarn ends into the back.

CROSS STITCHING. Work an oval design in centre of each block, following diagram and directions below left.

BLOCKING AND ASSEMBLING. Carefully block each piece so that all are the same size (approximately 23.5 cm by 31 cm). Lay out 10 blocks in 2 rows of 5 each, one row above the other, with all tops facing away from you. Using 1 long strand of blue and working from right to left, overcast adjacent top and bottom edges, taking yarn through each back loop only (see example of this technique, p. 46). Add on 3 more rows of 5 squares each until all squares are joined horizontally. Turn blanket sideways and join all the rows vertically.

WORKING THE BLANKET BORDER. With blue, work 2 rows of dc round the outside edge of the blanket, working 1 stitch in each stitch, 2 stitches in each corner, missing the overcast joining. Fasten off. Gently press.

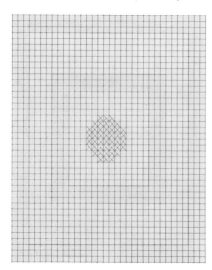

Each block is worked in basic Tunisian stitch, using this chart as a guide. A square in the chart equals 1 stitch and a row represents 2 rows of the pattern; there are 34 stitches and 84 rows. Though the cross stitch pattern in the centre appears to be off-balance, the motif, when finished, is actually centred because cross stitches are worked over the upright bars of the extra beige stitch.

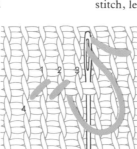
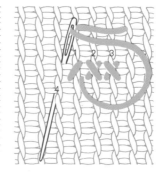

To make cross stitches, use a tapestry needle and one strand of blue yarn. Bring the needle up just below crossbars of stitch **1**; pull yarn through, leaving 10 cm at the back; take needle top to bottom behind both crossbars of stitch **2**, then behind crossbars of stitch **3**.

Work back across the same row, inserting the needle behind crossbars as before. To start the next row, weave needle down behind crossbars of stitch **4**; continue making rows of stitches until oval is complete; cut yarn; weave in ends. Stitches should not show on back.

Lacemaking

Needlepoint lace   **50**
Materials
Making a sampler   51
Needlepoint lace stitches   52
Meshes
Bars and picots   54
Insertions/Woven   55
Insertions/Russian   56
Edgings

Tatting   **57**
Terms and abbreviations
Materials
Tatting techniques   58
Forming the double stitch
Practice with one shuttle   59
Points to remember   60
Working with two threads   61

Filet lace netting   **62**
Materials and equipment
Making the basic knot   63
Basic mesh techniques   64
Plain square mesh/   65
Filet lace sampler
Embroidering the sampler   66
Filet lace cushion cover   67

Bobbin lace   **68**
Tools and materials
Preparing the pricking/   69
Bobbin lace sampler
Winding the bobbins   70
Working the two basic stitches
Weaving a design   71
Pinning within stitches
Ground patterns   72
Other lace techniques   73

Lace weaves   **74**
Materials
Setting up the loom   75
Preparing the weft
The weaves   76

Hairpin crochet lace   **78**
Making strips
Joining strips   79
Finishing edges
Variations

Nineteenth-century Belgian bobbin lace with needlepoint lace insertions, from the collection of Susanna E. Lewis, Brooklyn, New York.

Needlepoint lace

Introduction to needlepoint lace
Materials
Making a sampler
General information on stitches
Meshes
Bars and picots
Insertions/Woven
Insertions/Russian
Edgings
Needlepoint lace butterfly

Introduction

Needlepoint lace is what its name suggests – lace made with a needle and thread. The techniques probably evolved from those used for openwork embroidery, but the structure is built entirely of thread, with fabric used only as an anchoring device. While there are several styles of needlepoint lace, just one, called **Renaissance lace**, is dealt with in this chapter; it is not difficult to do. To produce this lace, variations of buttonhole stitch are worked between sections of a narrow tape that has been tacked, along the lines of the design, to a backing. When work is completed, the backing is removed, leaving just the lace structure.

Renaissance lace was popular in the Victorian era.

Materials

First consideration is usually given to selecting a tape, because the thread is then chosen to match or blend with it. For best performance, the tape should be between 5 mm and 1.5 cm wide, flexible enough to mould to curves in a design, constructed loosely enough so that it offers little resistance to a thick needle, and woven in a way that will guide the spacing of stitches. Braids, eyelets, tape with picot edging, and two ricracs twisted together are suitable possibilities. See examples on the right.

For the thread, medium-weight crochet cotton is recommended because it has the firm twist needed for these techniques and enough body to give character to the stitches. The needle should have an eye large enough to accommodate the thread; a tapestry needle is preferable because it will not catch in the backing. You will also need an ordinary needle and sewing thread for tacking, sturdy paper for backing, and fabric that contrasts with thread colour to show it up. A transfer pencil is useful because it allows you to hot-iron a design on to backing fabric. A thimble and small scissors are also necessary.

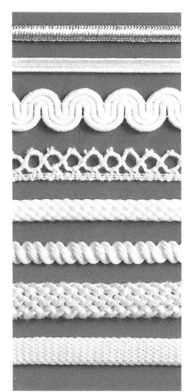

Making a sampler

A sampler is an easy and practical way to learn needlepoint lace techniques.

Materials

3.60 m of tape (see opposite page for suitable choices), 1 ball medium-weight crochet cotton, tapestry needle, tacking thread and needle, medium-weight drawing paper 28 by 35 cm, plain, smooth fabric, 28 by 35 cm, in colour to contrast with the thread.

Preparation

Cut 4 strips of tape 20 cm long, 3 strips 30 cm long, and a 1 m piece for the border. Lay fabric on the paper and strips on the fabric, arranging them so that the large centre spaces measure about 6.5 by 4.5 cm. Tack strips to

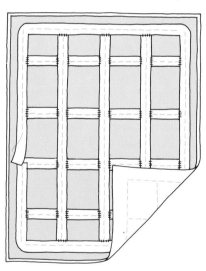

fabric and paper; oversew tapes to each other at intersections. Tack border over ends of strips, rounding the corners.

Working the stitches

Following key (above right), work stitches 1–37 in order. The number of rows to work is given with the stitch instructions on pp. 52–56. Where no number of rows is given, fill section as shown on right. Do not stitch into backing.

		37		
27	21 / 19 / 20A-B		15 / 16 / 17A / 17B	27
32	22	1 / 2 / 3	4	23 / 32
33	30	6 / 8 8 / 7	9 / 10 / 11	5 / 33
34	31	12 / 13 / 14	18	29 / 34
	28A	24 / 26 26	25	28B
	35	36	35	

KEY TO SAMPLER DIAGRAM

1. Single net stitch
2. Double net stitch
3. Buttonholed net stitch
4. Brussels net stitch
5. Pea stitch
6. Cloth stitch
7. Eyelets in cloth stitch
8. Embroidered cloth stitch
9. Side stitch
10. Double side stitch
11. Shell stitch
12. Spanish point
13. Twisted Spanish point
14. Twisted Spanish point patterns
15. Twisted bar
16. Double twisted bar
17A, B Buttonholed bars
18. Branched bar filling
19. Bar with buttonholed picot
20A, B Bar with pinned picots
21. Bar with bullion picot
22. Woven leaves
23. Open leaves with wheels
24. Beaded insertion
25. Wheel filling
26. Rings
27. Rosettes
28A, B Spiders' webs
29. Buttonholed Russian stitch
30. Double Russian stitch
31. Half bars
32. Knotted edging
33. Side stitch edging
34. Pinned picot edging
35. Bullion picot edging
36. Buttonholed picot edging
37. Shell edging

Needlepoint lace stitches

General information

All the stitches for Renaissance lace are variations of just one, buttonhole stitch, illustrated below in both right and left forms because most of the patterns are worked back and forth in rows. To produce such variety, the buttonhole stitch

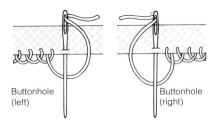

Buttonhole (left)   Buttonhole (right)

is worked three different ways: (1) loosely, referred to in directions as a loop; (2) tightly and closely spaced, called stitch or buttonholing; (3) to one side over another loop, known as sideways stitch. For more variety, buttonhole stitch may be combined with embroidery techniques, such as bullion knot or weaving. The page references for these are given where needed.

General rules for working

1. The stitches should be pulled firmly enough to prevent their sagging, but not so taut as to draw in the tape edges.
2. The tape edge is used as a guide in spacing the stitches and rows.

Oversewing

3. Oversewing stitch (illustration above) is used along tape edges between rows.
4. For a mesh stitch or filling, the number of loops remains constant for a regular space, is increased or decreased as needed for an irregular space, but stitch depth remains the same.
5. For most patterns with a one-row repeat, each row is started with a whole loop, and ended with a half-loop.

Meshes

Meshes are especially suitable for filling large or irregular spaces in a lace pattern. They are grouped here and opposite according to the basic way of working each stitch. *Net stitches* (this page) are openwork patterns, each a variation of the single net stitch (right). *Cloth stitches* (top row opposite) are closely spaced in a solid cloth effect; they can be embellished with eyelets or embroidery. *Side stitches* (centre row) are characterised by a second stitch that is made sideways over the first and locks it in place. *Spanish points* (bottom row) are similar to single net, but have an extra twist in the loop.

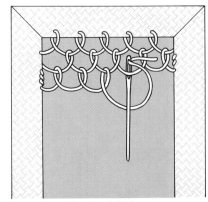

Single net stitch

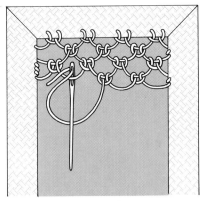

Double net stitch

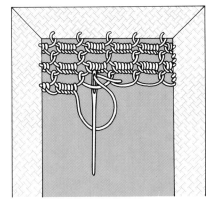

Buttonholed net stitch

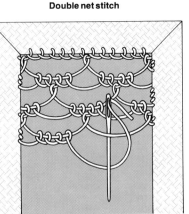

Brussels net stitch

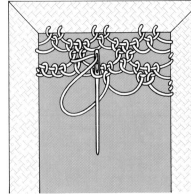

Pea stitch

Single net stitch (4 rows, No. 1). An open pattern, simplest and most basic of the meshes.
Row 1: work evenly spaced loops, making each loop about as deep as it is wide.
Row 2: repeat Row 1, working each stitch into the centre of the large loop above. Repeat this row for the pattern.

Double net stitch (5 rows, No. 2). This stitch looks better if you make the large loop a bit shallower than for the single net stitch (above).
Row 1: work 1 large loop and 1 small loop alternately.
Row 2: repeat Row 1, working large and small loops into each of the large loops above. Repeat this row for the pattern.

Buttonholed net stitch (8 rows, No. 3). This stitch is purposely started at the right edge because the second row, closely spaced buttonhole stitches, is easier to work from left to right. Also, it is evenly spaced, because it has a two-row repeat.
Row 1: working right to left, make widely spaced loops, beginning and ending with a half-loop.
Row 2: working left to right, fill each loop with closely spaced buttonhole stitches (about 6 for each full loop, 2 for each half-loop).
Row 3: working right to left, work large loops into the small spaces between buttonholed bars of the row above.
Repeat Rows 2 and 3 for pattern. For last row in sampler, catch tape between buttonholed bars.

Brussels net stitch (No. 4).
Row 1: make closely spaced loops in multiples of 6 (18 were made on the sampler).
Row 2: make 1 large loop into every sixth stitch above.
Row 3: make 4 stitches to form 3 loops on each large loop above.
Row 4: make 1 large loop into the centre of the 4-stitch group above.
Repeat Rows 3 and 4 for the pattern.

Pea stitch (No. 5).
Row 1: make 1 large loop and 1 small loop alternately, beginning and ending with half-loops.
Row 2: work 1 loop into the small loop above and 3 stitches forming 2 loops on each large loop, ending with 1 loop.
Row 3: make 2 stitches into the 3-loop group above (1 stitch between the first and second stitches, and 1 stitch between the second and third stitches).
Row 4: work 3 stitches on each large loop above and 1 stitch into the small loop.
Repeat Rows 3 and 4 for the pattern.

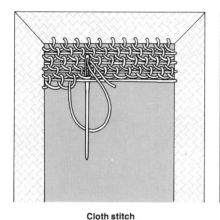

Cloth stitch

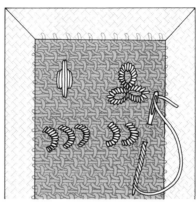

Eyelets in cloth stitch

Embroidered cloth stitch

Cloth stitch (12 rows, No. 6).
Row 1: working left to right, make closely spaced loops, then pull thread back across the space.
Row 2: again left to right, make a loop into each loop above, going over the loose thread as well. Pull thread back to left side and repeat this row.

Eyelets in cloth stitch (7 eyelets, No. 7).
Row 1: for each eyelet, miss 4 stitches, carrying thread straight across the empty space. At end of row, pull thread back to the left side.
Row 2: for each eyelet, work 3 buttonhole stitches over the 3 strands.

Embroidered cloth stitch (No. 8). Centre of the raised spot is 2 satin stitches worked over 1 cloth stitch and 4 rows; sides are 2 satin stitches over 1 cloth stitch and 2 rows. Leaves consist of 3 bullion knots; to hold it flat, each clover leaf is anchored with 1 stitch at centre of outside curve.

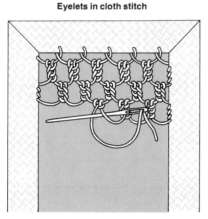

Side stitch

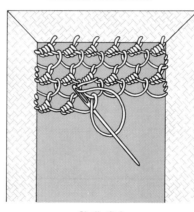

Double side stitch

Shell stitch

Side stitch (4 rows, No. 9).
Row 1: left to right, make 1 loose buttonhole stitch; make a second stitch sideways around both threads of first one; pull tightly in place.
Row 2: working right to left, and reversing position of thread, repeat Row 1.

Double side stitch (5 rows, No. 10).
Row 1: make single loops spaced widely apart.
Row 2: make 1 loose buttonhole stitch into loop above; make a second stitch in same loop; pull it tight. Make 2 sideways stitches below second buttonhole stitch. Repeat this row for pattern.

Shell stitch (6 rows, No. 11).
Row 1: working left to right, make 1 side stitch, pulling thread firmly so that the sideways stitch lies against the tape and the loop slants left. Make 3 more sideways stitches above first, each one slightly looser than preceding one. One shell is now completed; start next shell touching it.
Row 2: right to left, work 1 stitch between each shell, drawing loop thus formed closely under shell.

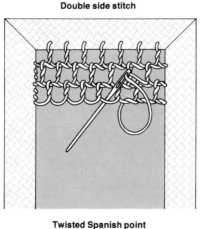

Spanish point

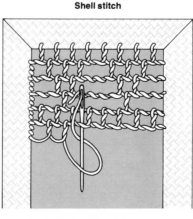

Twisted Spanish point

Twisted Spanish point patterns

Spanish point (4 rows, No. 12).
Row 1: left to right, make a thread loop that faces right; holding loop with left thumb, take needle through the tape (or stitch above), then through the loop; adjust stitch to desired depth.
Row 2: repeat Row 1, facing each loop to left.

Twisted Spanish point (2 rows, No. 13).
Row 1: work as for Row 1 in Spanish point.
Row 2: work back along row above; pass needle once behind bottom of each loop. Pull thread firmly, but not so tight as to pull bars askew.

Twisted Spanish point patterns (5 rows, No. 14). Arrange stitches as shown.

Needlepoint lace stitches

Bars and picots

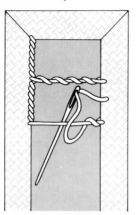

Twisted bar (No. 15).
Fasten thread to tape at the left side, stretch it across the space, and take a stitch in tape on opposite side. (When laying the foundation of a bar, stretch the thread firmly across the opening, but not so taut that you draw the tape inwards.) Work back to the left side, winding the thread 4 times around the bar (for a wider space, you would wind more times to make bar firm).

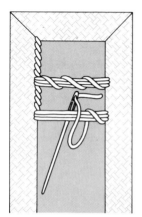

Double twisted bar (No. 16).
Lay a foundation across the space as for twisted bar on left, but stretch thread across 3 times instead of once. Work back to the left side, going over the bar 3 times. (Fewer twists are needed for this stitch to make it firm.)

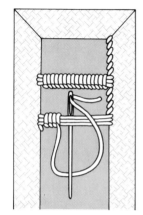

Buttonholed bar (No. 17A).
Starting at the right edge, stretch thread across the space 3 times for foundation, then work closely spaced buttonhole stitches across it. Before starting the stitches, oversew 1 space down on the tape to secure the end of the bar and prevent it from curling. For a thicker bar (No. 17B), make buttonhole stitches over 5 threads.

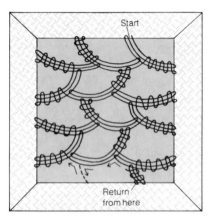

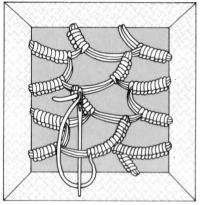

Branched bar filling (No. 18).
Each bar should emerge from last one without having to cut and join the thread. Starting in the upper right corner (see diagram), make a foundation of 3 threads; work buttonhole stitches for half its length. Make a new foundation for the next bar, anchoring it through bottom of the last stitch; work buttonhole stitches for half its length. Begin the third and subsequent bars the same way. When all bars have been laid out and partially buttonholed, complete them by working back along each one in reverse order.

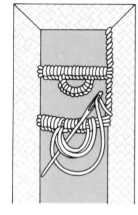

Bar with buttonholed picot (No. 19). Make a buttonholed bar, working stitches three-quarters of the way across, or 6 stitches beyond where the picot is to start. Take thread back to the left and pass needle between the sixth and seventh stitches, then back to the right and around the bar, then back to the left and between the same 2 stitches (there should be a 3-strand loop below the bar). Work closely spaced buttonhole stitches over the loop, then complete the bar.

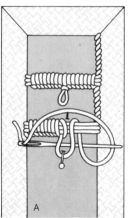
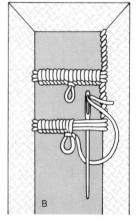
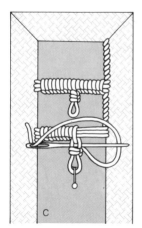

Bar with pinned picot (No. 20). Make a buttonholed bar, working stitches to the point where you want the picot; insert a pin into backing fabric to the desired depth of the picot. Pass thread around the pin, then behind the foundation threads to the outside of the loop. Make a side stitch around the loop and the working thread (as shown in illustration A). Complete the buttonholed bar (B). For a longer picot, make 2 or more side stitches, placing the first one down low enough for the additional stitches to fit between it and the bar (C). Take care not to sew backing.

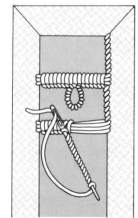

Bar with bullion picot (No. 21). Make a buttonholed bar, working stitches to the point where you want the picot; insert needle halfway through the last stitch that was made and wind thread around the needle point 15 times (not too tightly). Pull needle through and draw the bullion into a circle. Complete the buttonholed bar.

Insertions/Woven

Open leaves with wheels (No. 23). Stretch thread bottom to top and form 3 small leaves tied with a sideways stitch. Weave around the centre, going over side leaves, under stem and top leaf 4 times. Wind thread twice around stem before making next pair of leaves (A).

Woven leaves (No. 22). Form stem and 2 groups of leaves 2.5 cm apart (B), then retrace foundation, bottom to top, anchoring *through* each sideways stitch. Starting at top, weave first leaf tip to base, going over thread groups alternately on each side; weave stem and side leaves same way (C).

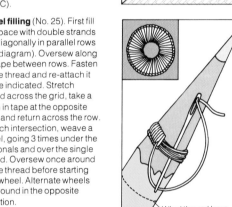

Beaded insertion (No. 24). Make 1 row of large, evenly spaced loops along each long side of the space (7 loops were made in the sampler). Starting at the top left side, connect opposite loops by taking the thread 4 times through each pair; be sure the thread does not become crossed or twisted. Before moving from one group to the next, oversew once around the left loop.

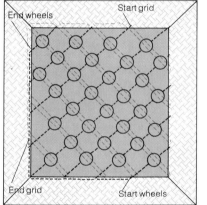

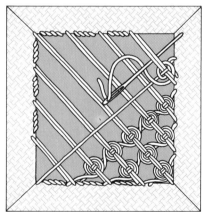

Wheel filling (No. 25). First fill the space with double strands laid diagonally in parallel rows (see diagram). Oversew along the tape between rows. Fasten off the thread and re-attach it where indicated. Stretch thread across the grid, take a stitch in tape at the opposite side, and return across the row. At each intersection, weave a wheel, going 3 times under the diagonals and over the single thread. Oversew once around single thread before starting next wheel. Alternate wheels are wound in the opposite direction.

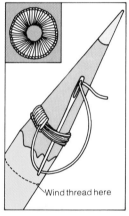

Rings (No. 26). These are made separately, then sewn on to the work wherever desired. Wind thread around a rubber pencil 15 times, then buttonhole over all the strands. (The buttonholing is easier if you push the threads up towards the pencil point.) When ring is complete, remove from pencil, flatten, and sew in place.

Wind thread here

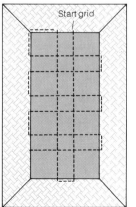

Rosette (No. 27). This appears in the sampler as one filling for a small space. It can also be worked in multiples to fill a larger area. First prepare a grid as in the diagram, laying 2 pairs of parallel strands for each rosette. Notice that the intersecting areas for each rosette are spaced 1 stitch apart and interlaced. For each rosette, weave a wheel, going around the circle 4 times, then buttonhole closely over all threads, placing 2 stitches between the parallel strands and 3 stitches at the corners.

Spiders' webs (No. 28A, No. 28B). This stitch is good for filling a square space. First make 4 twisted bars, 2 across the centre and 2 diagonally. Twist the fourth bar only to the centre, work spider's web, then complete the bar.

Woven web (No. 28A). Working from the centre out, weave a wheel, missing 1 bar at the end of each round so threads will alternate on each row.

Ridged web (No. 28B). Starting at the centre, take thread under 2 bars, then weave in a circle, going back over 1 bar, forward under 2 bars (backstitch).

55

Needlepoint lace stitches

Insertions/Russian

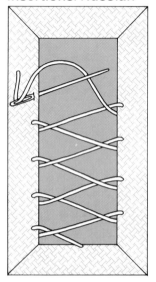

Basic Russian foundation

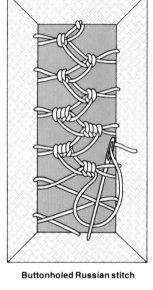

Buttonholed Russian stitch

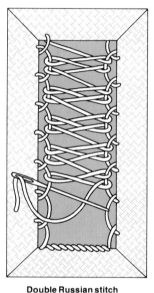

Double Russian stitch

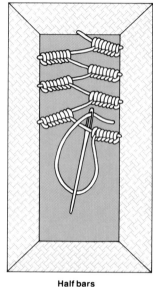

Half bars

Buttonholed Russian stitch (No. 29). Starting at bottom centre of the space, make a basic Russian foundation, looping thread from side to side as in first illustration, left (for sampler, there are 9 loops on each side). Take a small stitch at top centre to secure thread, then work down the centre of the foundation, making closely spaced buttonhole stitches over each pair of threads. Make 2 stitches over each of the first 4 pairs, 4 stitches over the next 5 pairs, 6 stitches over the next 4, and 8 stitches over the last 4 pairs.

Double Russian stitch (No. 30). Make 1 row of evenly spaced loops along the tape on each side of the space (for the sampler, 14 loops). Connect opposite pairs of loops with 2 Russian foundation stitches through each one. Density can be increased by taking 3 or 4 stitches in each loop.

Half bars (No. 31). Starting at the top centre, make 1 Russian foundation stitch on the right side and pull it up to a loose diagonal, take 1 stitch in the tape to secure the bar (not shown), then make 8 buttonhole stitches over the diagonal thread. Repeat this procedure on alternate sides.

Edgings

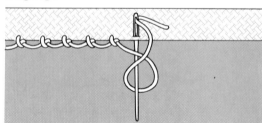

Knotted edging (No. 32). Make a loop as illustrated; take the needle through the tape edge, then through the loop, going behind the upper and over the lower thread. Work this and all the edgings on the sampler from left to right.

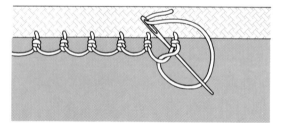

Side stitch edging (No. 33). Make a buttonhole loop on the tape; over this loop make 1 sideways stitch and pull it up close to the tape. Take the thread through the loop and then make another sideways stitch next to the first one.

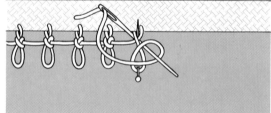

Pinned picot edging (No. 34). Make a buttonhole loop on the tape. Insert a pin into backing to desired depth of picot; take thread around it right to left. Make a second loop in front of the pin; pass the needle through buttonhole and second loop, pull thread tight.

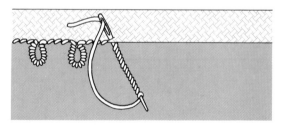

Bullion picot edging (No. 35). Oversew along the tape to desired place for picot. Insert needle halfway through tape, wind thread around needle point 15 times, draw bullion into a tight circle.

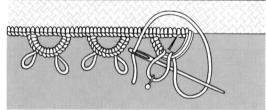

Buttonholed picot edging (No. 36). Work 7 buttonhole stitches along the tape edge. Make a buttonholed picot (see directions, p. 54), adding 1 pinned picot (p. 54) every 5 stitches, if desired.

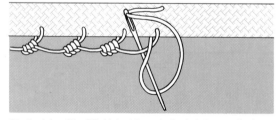

Shell edging (No. 37). Make 1 loose buttonhole loop on the tape; make a second stitch sideways around both threads of the first one and pull it tight. Make 3 more sideways stitches above the first.

Tatting

Introduction
Terms and abbreviations
Materials
Forming the double stitch
Practice with one shuttle
Points to remember
Working with two threads

Introduction

Tatting is a form of lacework that consists of one knot, called double stitch, worked in groups over a single thread. This thread is pulled to draw stitches into rings and chains, and these in turn are joined in larger groupings or motifs. Traditionally, the technique has been used to make edgings and insertions, but a tatting enthusiast can produce items such as collars or a table centre piece. This lace is usually worked with fine cotton thread, so it is delicate looking but very strong.

In tatting, a continuous thread is used and it is wound on a small shuttle (see below). A loop of thread is held in the left hand while the shuttle, held by the right, is manoeuvred around it; double stitches (the same knots are known as lark's head in macramé) form over the shuttle thread. To use the instructions in this section effectively, you should practise a double stitch (p. 58) until you can do it smoothly – and rapidly. Then try each technique in the order presented: they are arranged in order of increasing complexity.

For tatting directions, there are special terms and abbreviations. Those used in this book are listed on the immediate right. These are in common use elsewhere, except for slip join and lock join. Most patterns make no distinction between the two, but simply say 'join'.

Terms and abbreviations

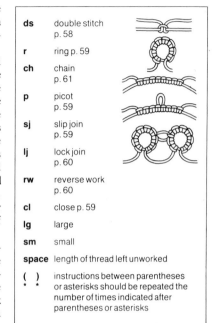

ds	double stitch p. 58	
r	ring p. 59	
ch	chain p. 61	
p	picot p. 59	
sj	slip join p. 59	
lj	lock join p. 60	
rw	reverse work p. 60	
cl	close p. 59	
lg	large	
sm	small	
space	length of thread left unworked	
( ) * *	instructions between parentheses or asterisks should be repeated the number of times indicated after parentheses or asterisks	

Materials

There are two types of tatting shuttles commonly available. One is metal with a removable bobbin and a hook for joining rings. This is best suited to fine crochet cotton in sizes No. 60 to 10. The other shuttle is plastic and has a centre post around which the thread is wound, and a tapered point to use in joining. It is more suitable for No. 5 or No. 3 (a thread thicker than No. 3 is impractical because you cannot wind enough on the bobbin). In addition, you might want a steel crochet hook to use instead of the shuttle point for joining, and needles for finishing thread ends (see p. 60).

The best thread for tatting is smooth cotton with a firm twist. Samples made with different thicknesses of thread are shown on the far right. For practice, No. 5 or 3 crochet cotton or thin string is best.

Plastic tatting shuttles.
Plain (left) for beginner.
With hook and bobbin
(right) for colours.

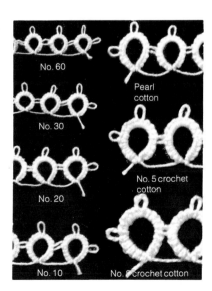

No. 60

No. 30

No. 20

No. 10

Pearl cotton

No. 5 crochet cotton

No. 5 crochet cotton

Tatting techniques

Forming the double stitch

Double stitch (ds) is the fundamental technique used in tatting. It is formed in two stages, with the right hand used to manoeuvre the shuttle around a loop of thread controlled by the left hand. It is this left-hand loop that forms the stitches over the shuttle thread. Once you grasp this principle, and master the forward and backward movement of the shuttle, co-ordination of the tatting movements is fairly easy and a steady rhythm can be established.

Preparing a bobbin. Wind thread firmly from centre to edge of bobbin; insert bobbin in the shuttle.

Holding the thread. Unwind 40 cm; hold the end firmly between thumb and index finger of left hand. Spread your fingers, wind thread around them, and grasp thread again after it comes full circle. Hold shuttle horizontally in right hand, with thread unwinding from the back, passing over the top of the hand and supported by raising the little finger (A).

First half of double stitch. Holding the thread as shown, pass shuttle *under* the top thread of loop held in left hand (B). Still holding shuttle horizontally, slide it backwards *over* the same thread (C). Allow thread to slide off the right hand and pull shuttle thread taut. At the same time, relax fingers of the left hand slightly, so that the *loop forms around the shuttle thread* (D).

Second half of double stitch. Hold the shuttle horizontally as before, but instead of passing thread over the right hand, push down on it with the fingers. Pass the shuttle *over* the top thread of the left-hand loop (E), then slide it backwards *under* this thread (F). Pull shuttle thread taut, allowing *loop to transfer to the shuttle thread* (G). If the stitch has been formed correctly, you should be able to slide the shuttle thread through it. Practise until actions are automatic.

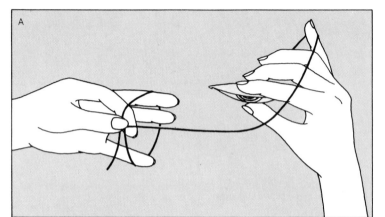

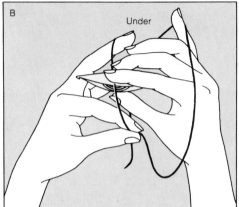

Under

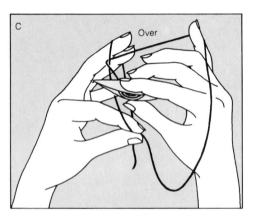

Over

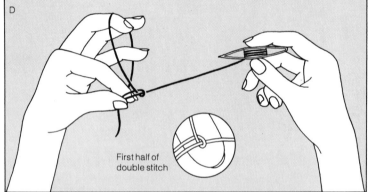

First half of double stitch

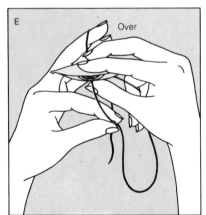

Over

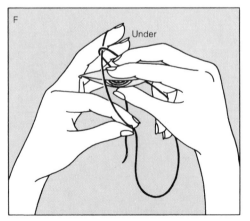

Under

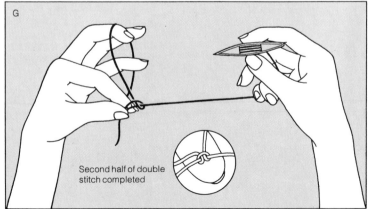

Second half of double stitch completed

Practice with one shuttle

Two of the basic elements in tatting are **rings** and **picots**. These should be mastered along with the **slip join** technique (bottom of page) before you proceed to the more complex methods that follow.

A 'ring' is a circle, semicircle or oval of double stitches formed by pulling on the shuttle thread. Its size and shape can vary depending on the number of stitches, the thickness of the thread and how tight the shuttle thread is pulled.

A picot is a thread loop set between two stitches. It is used for decoration and to join rings. Picot size, too, can be varied, but should be consistent in one pattern, unless picots of different sizes are called for in the directions. As a rule, small picots (3 to 5 mm long) are used for joining rings; large picots (5 mm or longer) are used to enhance a design.

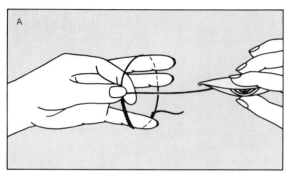

A ring (r) is formed by releasing left-hand loop with which double stitches are made, and pulling on the shuttle thread until stitches are drawn into a tight circle (see above) or semicircle. In instructions this is called *closing* (cl).

To practise making a ring, wind thread around left hand and work 20 ds (A), slide thread off left hand, and, holding the stitches between left thumb and index finger, pull shuttle thread gently so that stitches are drawn together. Keep pulling until stitches are as closely set as possible (C).

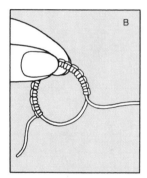

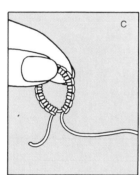

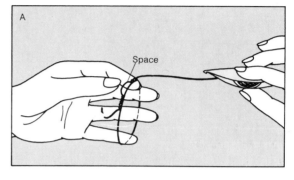

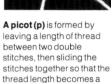

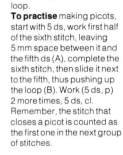

A picot (p) is formed by leaving a length of thread between two double stitches, then sliding the stitches together so that the thread length becomes a loop.

To practise making picots, start with 5 ds, work first half of the sixth stitch, leaving 5 mm space between it and the fifth ds (A), complete the sixth stitch, then slide it next to the fifth, thus pushing up the loop (B). Work (5 ds, p) 2 more times, 5 ds, cl. Remember, the stitch that closes a picot is counted as the first one in the next group of stitches.

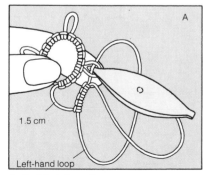

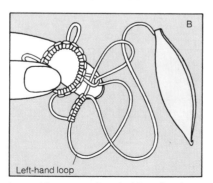

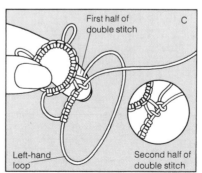

A slip join (sj), made by working a double stitch through an adjacent picot, is the conventional method of joining two rings. **For practice,** make r of 20 ds and 3 p, as explained above right.

Leave 1.5 cm space (length of thread) and start second r with 5 ds (A). Lay the third p of the first r over the left-hand loop. Using tip of shuttle or a crochet hook, draw up a loop through the p and

pass shuttle through this loop (B). Keeping shuttle thread taut, pull loop close to last ds, taking care not to pull shuttle thread back through the picot (C). The join counts as first half of a ds;

complete the second half (see inset) and count this as the first ds in the next group. Finish r with (5 ds, p) twice, 5 ds, cl. Repeat second r as many times as desired to produce a handsome edging.

Tatting techniques

Practice with one shuttle

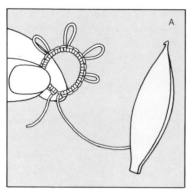

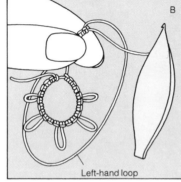

Left-hand loop

Reversing work (rw) is the turning of a completed ring downwards, so that the next ring is worked above the previous ring. This technique permits a greater variety in design, and also allows you to make wider patterns.

To practise reversing, make this tatted braid.

Make r of 5 ds, sm p, (3 ds, lg p) 3 times, 3 ds, sm p, 5 ds, cl (A); rw, 5 mm space, make second r like the first (B), rw, 5 mm space, make third r of 5 ds, sj to fifth p of first ring, 3 ds, lg p, (3 ds, lg p) twice, 3 ds, sm p, 5 ds, cl. Repeat instructions for the third ring until braid is the desired length, joining each ring to the fifth picot of the ring adjacent to it.

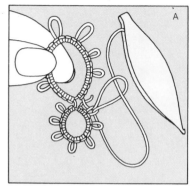

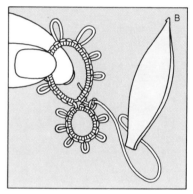

Locking join (lj) is the connecting of two parts with half a slip join. Once made, shuttle thread can no longer be pulled through stitches, so method is limited to completed rings or chains.

To practise locking join, make this medallion.

Make centre r of (2 ds, sm p) 7 times, 2 ds, cl; starting next to last ds of centre r, make petal of r of 5 ds, sm p, 3 ds, sm p, (3 ds, lg p) 3 times, (3 ds, sm p) twice, 5 ds, cl; lj to centre r by drawing up a loop through first p, passing shuttle through this loop (A), then pulling the loop tight (B). Do not count lj as a stitch. Make 7 more petals as follows: r of 5 ds, sj to last p of previous petal, 3 ds, sj to next p, (3 ds, lg p) 3 times, (3 ds, sm p) twice, 5 ds, cl; lj to next p in centre r. Join 8th ring to 2nd and 1st p of 1st r.

Points to remember

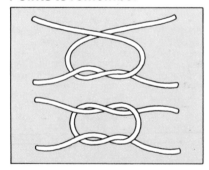

A new thread is joined only at the end of a ring or chain, before starting the next part of the design. A reef knot, illustrated, is an effective way to tie threads together. Leave enough length so that the thread ends can be woven into the back of the completed work.

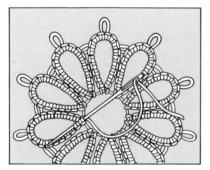

A thread end is finished most neatly by weaving it under a few stitches, then cutting the remainder. The needle used must have an eye large enough for the thread but thin enough to pass under stitches. An alternative is to run the thread up and down along the edge and pull tight.

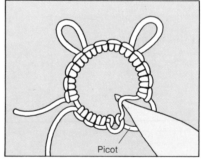

Picot

A mistake is corrected most easily while a ring is in progress. If it is necessary to open a ring, you have a better chance of success if you pry loose a thread between two stitches of a picot, as illustrated. Otherwise, thread must be cut, then rejoined after eliminating the error.

To avoid confusion, remember:

1. The thread in the left hand is the one to show itself in the stitches; if it is looped, the result will be a ring; if it is passed over the fingers, the result will be a chain.

2. Work progresses from left to right.

3. The knotted edge of the double stitches are facing to the left while a ring or chain is being formed.

4. The term *picot* refers only to a thread loop, not to the double stitch that encloses it. The closing stitch is counted as the first in the next group of stitches.

5. Never set work down in the middle of a ring or chain; it is difficult to resume the correct position and tension.

Working with two threads

Working with two threads considerably enlarges the scope of tatting. It permits introduction of a second colour, and allows you to work stitches over the connecting threads between rings – a form called **chain (ch)**. To make a chain, one thread is passed over the left fingers and around the little finger to provide tension; the second is used to make double stitches. As with a ring, thread in the left hand forms the stitches.

For working two threads of one colour, use a shuttle plus ball of thread and work over the ball thread to form chains. Tatting with two colours usually requires two shuttles.

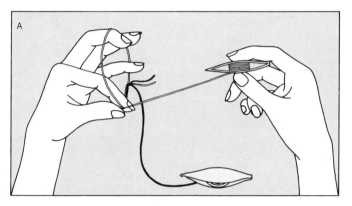

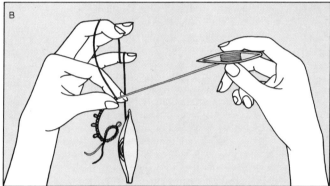

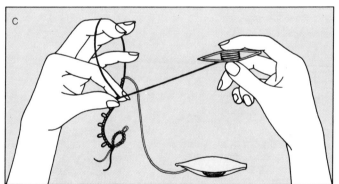

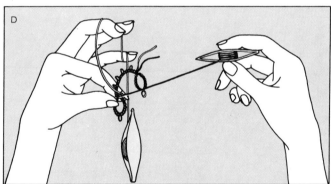

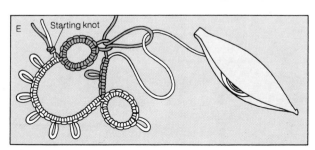

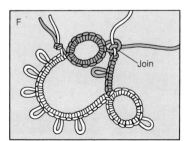

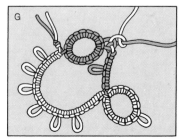

Two-colour edging. Composed of rings and chains in two colours, this is a good practice piece for mastering the use of two shuttles. Keep in mind that the shuttle not in use rests in the lap or on a table, and whatever colour is in the left hand will form the stitches. Wind one shuttle with blue, the other with white; knot the two ends loosely together. Starting close to knot, **with blue**, make r of 8 ds, p, 8 ds (A), cl, rw; **with white** tensioned over left hand and blue in right hand, make ch of (3 ds, p) 6 times, 6 ds (B), do not rw; **with white**, make r of 8 ds, p, 8 ds (C), rw; **with blue** tensioned over left hand and white in right hand, start ch with 3 ds, p, 3 ds (D), sj to p of 1st blue r as follows: pull up a loop of blue, insert white shuttle through it (E), pull loop close to the last ds (F), and complete sj (G), finish ch with (3 ds, p) 3 times, 3 ds, rw; **with white**, make r of 8 ds, sj to p of 1st white r, 8 ds, cl, rw; **with blue**, make ch of (3 ds, p) 5 times, 3 ds, rw; make 2 more sm white rings, connecting them to p of first white r and with a blue ch between them, do not rw; **with white**, make ch of 6 ds, sj to 1st p of opposite white ch, 3 ds, sj to next p, (3 ds, p) 4 times, 3 ds, rw; **with blue**, make r of 8 ds, sj to 2nd p of last blue ch, 8 ds, cl. First repeat is now complete. To begin the next one, do not rw, but make 1st blue r right next to last one, rw; begin 1st white ch with 3 ds, sj to 1st p on opposite ch, finish with (3 ds, p) 5 times, 6 ds. Continue as for first repeat.

Filet lace netting

What is filet lace netting?
Materials and equipment
Making the basic knot
Basic mesh techniques
Plain square mesh/Filet lace sampler
Embroidering the sampler
Filet lace cushion cover

What is filet lace netting?

Filet lace netting is a type of netting used for many items, from tennis nets and hammocks to lace of the delicate kind shown on the right. No matter what form the netting takes, the basic technique remains the same and involves only one knot (see opposite page).

In lacemaking terms, filet netting is a mesh worked in diamond or square shape, with a design embroidered on it. (Actually, all mesh is diamond-shaped; it is squared as explained on p. 65).

Netting reached its peak of popularity in 17th-century Europe, when it featured intricate embroidery in many colours and textures. It came back into favour during the Victorian era, but in a less ornate form characterised by geometric patterns in natural-coloured cotton and linen thread. Our example shows this more moderate style, the one associated most closely with the tradition. Today, tradition can be followed with fine crochet cottons. Bear in mind, however, that the knots should look crisp and be nearly invisible; this requires smooth, tightly twisted cord (but not so hard a twist that knots will be obvious). Embroidery thread can be crochet cotton or stranded cotton.

Example of filet lace netting in which both beginning mesh and embroidery are worked in natural colours.

Diamond mesh

Square mesh

Materials and equipment

Besides knotting cord, you need heavier cord (about 30 cm) for a **foundation loop**, into which the starting meshes are made; a **shuttle** to hold knotting cord; and a **mesh stick** to establish mesh size. The number of starting meshes depends on the shape: several for diamond mesh, which starts at an edge (see facing page and p. 64); two for square mesh, which begins at a corner (p. 55). The ideal shuttle for lace is the netting needle below; an alternative, also shown, is two 15 cm upholsterer's needles placed in opposite directions and taped together below the eyes. A good mesh 'stick' for lace is a double-pointed knitting needle. The size of the needle will determine the size of the netting holes.

The best shuttle for lace is this special netting needle, made for the knotting of fine mesh.

An alternative shuttle can be made of two 15 cm upholsterer's needles, facing in opposite directions and taped together below the eyes.

Good mesh 'stick' for filet netting is a double-pointed knitting needle: slim enough to establish small openings, short enough to be manageable.

Making the basic knot

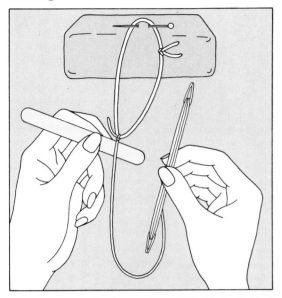

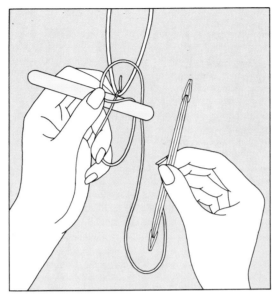

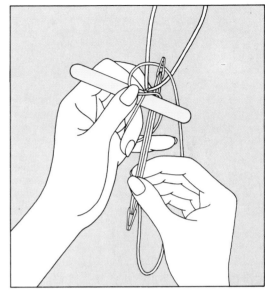

Knot foundation cord into loop; anchor to stable object so it will not move when pulled. Thread shuttle; be sure, when wound, it is not larger than mesh stick. Knot end of shuttle thread into foundation cord. Holding mesh stick between thumb and index finger of left hand and shuttle in right, as shown, pass shuttle thread over stick, around the third finger, and back up behind stick. Holding thread against stick with thumb, loop thread up and around figure-eight style. Pass shuttle through loop on finger, behind stick, through foundation loop, and over top of figure-eight loop.

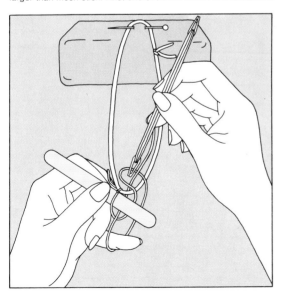

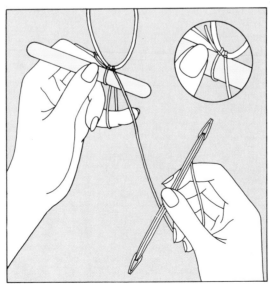

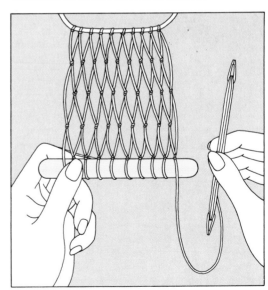

Draw shuttle through and away, *hooking trailing thread on little finger*. Release thumb, then loop on third finger; continue pulling until all slack tightens around stick, but *do not release thread on little finger*. Place knot on top of and touching stick, then release little finger, drawing thread towards you and keeping foundation cord taut. This forms first knot. Make starting loops on stick and over foundation (about 10 for diamond mesh above; for square mesh, see p. 65). Remove stick; turn work (knotting always goes left to right). Continue knotting, except now into loop above.

Filet lace netting

Basic mesh techniques

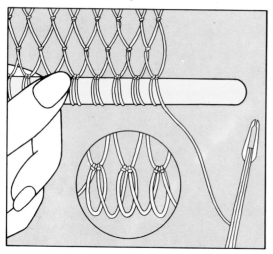

Shaping is accomplished by increasing (left) to widen the mesh, and decreasing (right) to narrow it. These drawings show the basic techniques; for the method used in making square mesh, refer to the opposite page. **To increase**, form two or more knots in one loop, widening that row, and also those that follow, since you will be knotting into an additional mesh wherever an increase was made.

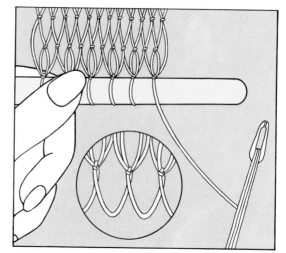

To decrease, work one knot in two or more loops, tying them together, and reducing the number of meshes to be worked in subsequent rows. Though shaping is the main use for both these techniques, especially by a beginner, decorative netting can be made by alternating decreases and increases from row to row, or at fixed intervals.

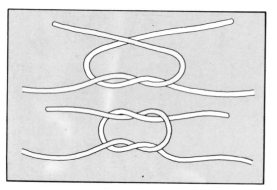

A new thread is best joined at the end of a row. Tie the end of the new thread very close to the last knot that was made, then join the two ends in a reef knot as shown. Clip the ends close to the joining knot.

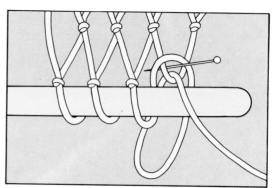

Try to correct mistakes before the knot is tightened. Use a pin to loosen it. If a knot cannot be untied, cut the thread close, untie it, and join a new thread. If you make very tight knots, whole sections of netting can be cut without knots coming undone.

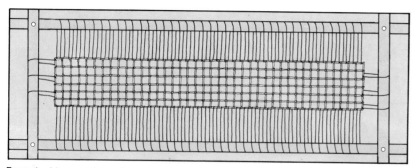

For embroidery, mesh must be stretched in a frame. Be sure to leave at least 3 cm allowance between mesh and inner edge of frame. Wind cord through each mesh and around the frame at top and bottom and through every other mesh at sides. Adjust tension so stretching is even and netting is taut. A mesh too long for a frame can be rolled up and the rolled part finished after the first is completed.

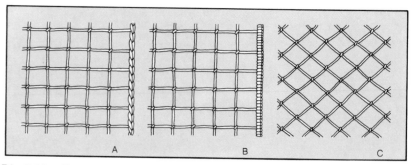

Edge finishes. For any technique, use the same thread as was used for the mesh. In square mesh, the shaping causes side meshes to come out double; to conceal this, and produce a straight, firm edge, good finishing choices are double crochet (A) or close buttonhole stitch (B). The edges of diamond mesh are often cut close to the knots (C). There is no danger of the knots coming undone.

Plain square mesh/Filet lace sampler

The square mesh being made at the bottom of the page is the beginning of the sampler-insertion below (the embroidery directions are on the next page). The directions produce a rectangular mesh approximately 5 by 40 cm, enough for the embroidery charted:

2 repeats, each 32 meshes (about 15 cm) long, *plus* an additional final triangular shape for balance, *plus* 6 extra meshes at each end – 83 meshes in all. To make a longer strip, add multiples of 32 meshes.

Though the quantities are specifically for the sampler, the technique applies to any square mesh. The progression will be easier to grasp if you remember that the work is turned for each new row.

All work is done with size 20 crochet cotton: the mesh in ecru; embroidery in ecru or white as directed. You also need a mesh stick (or knitting needle, size 2.75 or 2.25 mm); a steel netting needle (or a pair of 15 cm upholsterer's needles facing in opposite directions and taped together – see p. 62); a frame to stretch mesh for embroidery; tapestry needle for working embroidery.

One repeat

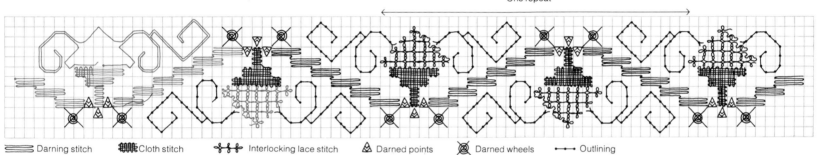

〰 Darning stitch   ▦ Cloth stitch   ✦ Interlocking lace stitch   △ Darned points   ⊗ Darned wheels   •—• Outlining

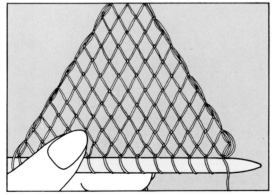

To begin a square mesh. Make two knots in foundation loop; turn work. Starting with second row, *increase one knot in each row* (put two knots in last loop) until you have enough knots for the width. The right-hand edge becomes sampler width (13 knots, 12 meshes).

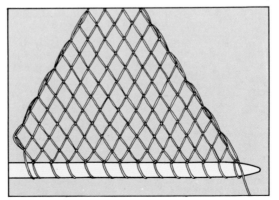

To make straight sides. On next row, *decrease one knot* (knot last two loops together); on following row, *increase one knot* (put two knots in last loop). *Alternate these rows* until long side of mesh is the desired length. In the sampler, this is 83 meshes.

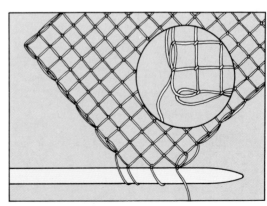

To square the last corner. Beginning with the next row after the length has been established, *decrease one knot at the end of each row* until two loops are left. Knot these two together and cut the threads close. Remove the foundation loop.

65

Filet lace stitches

Embroidering the sampler

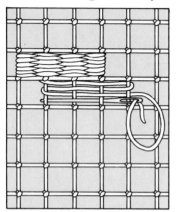

1. Darning stitch (ecru, single thread). In 1st group at left end, tie thread to top left corner of 1st mesh of design. Weave over and under meshes, from top to bottom, until space is filled – 10-12 threads will usually be enough. With next section, attach thread to left corner of 1st mesh, and proceed downwards.

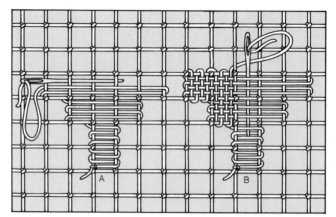

2. Cloth stitch (ecru, single thread). Done in two steps – first warp, then weft threads, in each pattern area. (A) Attach thread at bottom left. Weave single meshes first, over and under, bottom to top, 4 threads per mesh. Weave somewhat loosely; slack is taken up in second step. At next mesh, be sure to weave 1st thread as you did last thread on previous mesh; thread between will be included in next step. (B) Without breaking thread, begin at upper left and weave weft threads back and forth across warp threads. Include all intervening mesh threads in weaving; put in 4 threads per mesh. After each row, pull slightly on warp threads so that weaving is flat and even.

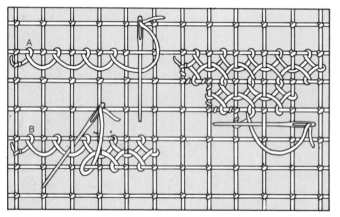

3. Interlocking lace stitch (white, single thread). Done in loop or buttonhole stitch; can be worked diagonally as well as back and forth. Each row takes two steps. (A) Begin with longest row on chart. Attach thread to centre of mesh on left side. Make one loop stitch in each mesh, large enough to cover half the mesh. At end of row, make a loop stitch in side of mesh. (B) Going right to left in same row, make loops as before, going over each loop in preceding row and under each vertical mesh. To move to second row, oversew around last mesh; begin again as in A, but pass needle through bottom loops of previous row to interlock.

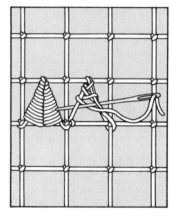

4. Darned points (white, single thread). Darn from top to base. Begin with left point. Attach thread at lower left corner of mesh. Loop around top, down to opposite corner, back up to top. This forms a scaffold for darning. Beginning at top, darn alternately from each side into centre – from right a buttonhole stitch, from left a plain stitch; catch in loose end from knot as part of scaffold. When working last stitch on each side, go around bottom of mesh to anchor base of point. Run thread behind mesh to centre top of next point and form scaffold as before.

5. Darned wheels (ecru, single thread). Attach thread at centre of 4 meshes. Make a bar from there to each corner of 4-mesh square by passing thread around corner, then passing needle twice around it to twist bar. When bars are made, weave thread spirally around centre, over bars and under mesh threads, until wheel is desired size (about four times). Fasten off on back by passing thread through twists of a bar or tying a reef knot with beginning thread.

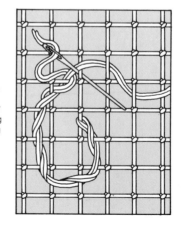

6. Outlining (white, double thread). Begin at bottom centre of interlocking lace stitch; weave over and under mesh threads as indicated by dots on chart. Following chart and photograph, weave first spiral. When centre is reached, begin weaving back alongside first thread, except pass thread *under* each mesh thread previously passed *over* and twisting once around previously laid thread. Continue around second spiral, then finish off top of first on way back to triangle. Continue around triangle, making other side the same. Fasten off thread with reef knot to beginning thread.

Filet lace cushion cover

Materials

Small netting shuttle; knitting needle, 2.25 mm, for mesh stick; tapestry needle; embroidery scissors; frame and cord to mount mesh (at least 30 cm square inside space); size 20 crochet cotton, 1 ball, ecru; size 8 pearl cotton, 1 ball each, 5 shades of blue; square cushion for the finished piece. It is 56 meshes (about 25.5 cm) square; for a larger size, use size 10 crochet cotton, size 2.75 or 3 mm knitting needle, size 5 pearl cotton.

Making the net (square mesh)

To begin, make two knots into foundation loop; turn. Starting with second row, *increase* one knot at end of each row until you have 57 knots. On next row, net plain (no increase). Next row, begin *decreasing* one knot at end of each row

until two knots are left. Knot these together, cut thread, remove foundation loop. Stretch mesh in frame, winding the cord through every other mesh.

Embroidery

In five shades of blue, charted as A, B, C, D, E (lightest to darkest). Stitches are those in sampler, but worked as listed on this page. To secure thread ends during work, run thread back and forth a few times from back (do not make knots). Always thread needle with thread as it comes off the ball or skein, this enhances sheen of stitches and keeps thread from untwisting. Turn frame with stretched mesh so the raised mesh threads run vertically and face you; those on the back run horizontally. Direction of raised threads makes a difference in the darning stitches.

A traditional design adapted for the present day as a cushion cover. The fish is the carp, a favourite in Chinese folklore, worked in five shades of blue on an ecru mesh. The cushion cover is 56 meshes (about 25.5 cm) square, but can easily be made larger by changing thread and mesh stick (knitting needle) sizes.

Cloth stitch (fish's outline and head). Numbers on diagram mark starting points for first threads. Follow lines to point where thread turns and second threads are woven in. Weave second threads in as far as possible, then begin at next number before completing first area. Lay in 4 threads per mesh; remember that first thread in each mesh is woven the same as last thread of previous mesh. Travelling threads, sometimes needed to get from one row to next, are incorporated into mesh threads during second stage of weaving. Work numbers 1-3 in colour A. Complete work in this colour before going further. Numbers 5-10 are worked in colour B, number 11 in colour C.

Darning stitch (fish's fins, tail bars and eye; all darkest areas in border). Lay in about 12 threads per mesh. Work bars in tail vertically in colour B (4). Raised vertical threads of mesh help 'outline' them. Go from bar to bar by passing thread through edge of cloth stitch from back. All other darning is worked horizontally. Fins on left side are worked in colours B and A in that order. Small bars are made after last row is completed by passing thread 3 times around mesh, then wrapping twice around threads and going to next small bar. Fins above head are worked, bottom to top, in colour D. When top mesh is completed, pull end of thread down so it is doubled, and proceed with outline at top of each fin. Work darning in eye, all border darning, in colour E.

Darned wheels (fish's eye; border). Worked somewhat differently from sampler. Thread is brought out from darned area adjacent at corner between first two wheels. Diagonal bars are laid

from centre to each corner, but first corner will have only one thread. Its second thread is laid after wheel itself is darned, enabling you to begin second wheel from adjacent corner. After second wheel is completed, thread is concealed in darning and brought around between next two wheels to be worked. In these wheels, corner threads are laid under mesh; darning is done by passing needle over mesh threads and under corner about 3 times. Work fish's eye in colour A, border wheels in D.

Interlocking lace stitch (fish's body; border). Work fish's body in colour A. Begin in upper left corner and work down. Conceal travelling threads in edge stitches at left side. Work outside border areas in colour E; begin and end at point indicated. Work inside border area in colour C; begin above fish's head and work first row all the way around, putting in diagonal stitches as indicated. Diagram shows how to lay in return row on diagonal (pass needle under mesh knot in same way that you pass it under mesh thread when doing a straight row).

Darned points (fish's teeth). Work in colour D, left to right. Scaffold for each point will have one thread on left, two on right.

Outlining (fish's eye, around head; inside border). Use double thread. Outline fish's eye in colour A, eye socket in D; top of head, from last tooth to first fin, in colour B; bottom of head, from tooth to halfway around back of head, in colour A; inside border in colour D.

Edging. With double thread in colour C, work 4 buttonhole stitches into each mesh all around (one extra at each corner).

A □ B □ C ▨ D ▨ E ▨

Bobbin lace

Introduction
Tools and materials
Preparing the pricking/Bobbin lace sampler
Winding bobbin pairs
Working the basic (half and whole) stitches
Weaving a design
Pinning within a design
Ground patterns
Other lace techniques

Introduction

This section shows the continental method for making bobbin lace, simplified for beginners. Bobbin lace is a lace woven of pairs of threads wound on bobbins. Only two basic stitches are involved, half stitch and whole stitch (see pp. 70–72), but from these many designs can be woven. The weaving is done over an actual-size paper pattern mounted on a pillow or padded board (see below). Pins are inserted through the pattern into the pillow to hold threads in place; the pattern is called a *pricking* because the design lines are perforated.

Bobbin lace is an old technique, dating back to the 15th century. As its popularity spread, local styles developed with patterns and stitches whose names reflected their place of origin. As a result, old pieces of bobbin lace exhibit a wide range of styles, from geometric patterns made with a few pairs of bobbins, to complex floral and pictorial designs requiring hundreds.

Russian braid

Cluny

Honiton

Examples of torchon

Scandinavian (free-form)

Tools and materials

Though their forms may be different, the elements required for bobbin lace have stayed the same for centuries: appropriate thread, bobbins, a pattern to follow, a pillow on which to mount the pattern. Traditional threads were silk, metallic or linen, spun very smooth and incredibly fine; for most modern bobbin lace, the choice is a smooth cotton. Bobbins were wood, bone or ivory, often weighted ('spangled') with glass beads to help hold thread taut. These bobbins can still be found in antique shops, but modern plastic and turned wooden bobbins are available. There are many satisfactory alternatives: slotted clothes pegs; dowelling or pencils cut to 15 cm lengths and grooved at one end; swizzle sticks; tapestry or fly shuttle bobbins used in weaving. Traditional prickings were of parchment so they could be re-used; for present purposes, use graph paper. The pillow or board must support the work firmly and take pins easily. A sawdust-filled cushion is ideal.

Lace pillow showing pocket (see p. 74) being made. Traditional antique and modern bobbins are being used. A pincushion is attached at the side to provide pins as the knots are made.

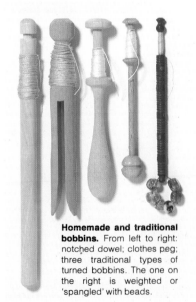

Homemade and traditional bobbins. From left to right: notched dowel; clothes peg; three traditional types of turned bobbins. The one on the right is weighted or 'spangled' with beads.

Preparing the pricking/Bobbin lace sampler

The sampler is designed to introduce you to the half stitch and whole stitch, and several of the patterns that can be made from them; and to the pattern, or pricking, that you follow to produce bobbin lace designs. On your graph paper (see equipment list on right), using waterproof ink, copy the diagram below square for square, putting in all dots, lines and numbers precisely as shown. One colour is sufficient; three are used here to make the diagram easier to follow. The right side of the braid-tape that edges the sampler is exactly the reverse of the pattern for the left side.

Pin your pricking at the corners, in the centre and as near the top of the pillow or board as possible. Using a pricker (a pin vice with a No. 8 needle), or a large needle fitted with a dowel or penholder handle, punch holes through all dots into the board.

The diagram is labelled with the names of the stitches in the order in which they are worked in the sampler, and the numbers of the pages on which instructions for them appear. You may find it helpful to indicate these stitch names on your diagram, perhaps also the page numbers. Listed below are abbreviations used in the instructions, and some working suggestions.

Abbreviations used in instructions

h st (or **t,c**)	half stitch	**c**	cross
w st (or **c,t,c**)	whole stitch	**pr,**	pair,
t	twist	**prs**	pairs

Points to remember

1. Pairs of bobbins are numbered left to right; numbers refer to their position on the board, not to actual bobbins.
2. In twisting, the right partner crosses over the left partner.
3. In crossing, the right bobbin of the left pair crosses over the left bobbin of the right pair.
4. Pins are placed perpendicular to the pillow or board, except at the edges where they are slanted outwards.
5. Place pins in their holes *between* the last two pairs of bobbins worked.
6. Always keep bobbins hanging evenly.
7. Do not roll bobbins on the board; this makes thread unwind. Instead, push them back and forth in pairs.
8. Join a new thread by working both new and old ends into the weaving together; clip when lace is completed.

Equipment specifically for sampler:

Board or 'pillow' approximately 65 cm square (usable also for project, p. 74). You can make your own with two or more pieces of corrugated cardboard taped together and padded with layers of felt, cotton or wool fabric. Acoustic tile or similar soft board will also work well, provided the surface is smooth. Insert a few pins in 'pillow' to be sure they go in easily and hold firmly. If they protrude at the bottom when pushed in all the way, place thick towelling or some similar padding underneath, or change to a shorter type of pin.

Dressmaker's straight pins (or shorter pins if they are more suitable) to use in weaving. Long T-pins are helpful for pinning bobbins not in use out of the way.

Bobbins, 24, either the traditional style (available in some shops) or one of the alternatives described in the list of materials on the opposite page.

Thread of almost any kind can be used in contemporary work. For learning, a smooth medium-weight crochet cotton is best. Sampler calls for one ball of size 10 in white or ecru.

Pricker, or a needle-like equivalent that will make satisfactory pinholes, for perforating the pricking at all the dots in the design. These are the points at which pins will be inserted, and piercing makes insertion far easier.

Pricking requires two 22 by 28 cm sheets of centimetre graph paper.

Crochet hook, size 4, 3.75 or 3.50 mm, which is used in making sewing joins (see p. 73).

Cloth cover, a 40 to 50 cm square of smooth fabric to protect lace that has been woven as you work on another section, or to cover your project when you put it aside or away.

Dowel, 3 mm in diameter and about 18 cm long, for mounting bobbins so that the sampler is ready for hanging when it is completed.

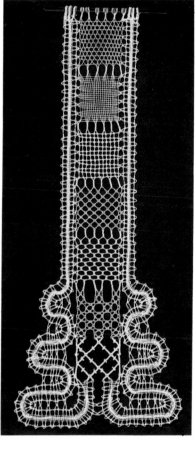

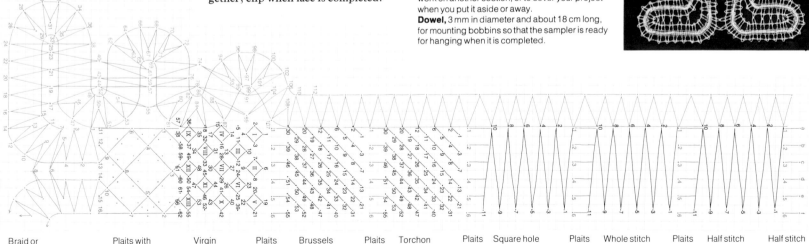

| Braid or tape p. 73 | Plaits with picots p. 73 | Virgin ground p. 72 | Plaits | Brussels ground p. 72 | Plaits | Torchon ground p. 72 | Plaits | Square hole ground p. 72 | Plaits | Whole stitch ground p. 72 | Plaits | Half stitch ground p. 72 | Half stitch plaits p. 70 |

Bobbin lace techniques

Winding bobbin pairs

Measure off enough thread to fill the bobbins but not overload them. For the sampler, this is about 6 metres – 3 m per bobbin. Wind bobbins from each end towards centre, leaving about 45 cm

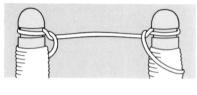

unwound for mounting. Secure thread with noose, made by looping thread as

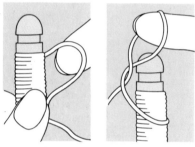

shown, twisting bobbin away from you, then slipping noose over head of bobbin. Pull thread to tighten. Noose lets you unwind thread as needed (above left) or wind up excess thread (right) without undoing the knot. Mount two pairs of bobbins together with a lark's head knot. Place a pin between each two pairs, just under dowel – points a to f on pricking.

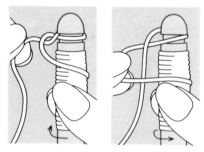

Working the basic (half and whole) stitches

The illustrations below show two bobbin pairs mounted as described on the left. Work is done on the side shown; the reverse side becomes the right side when lace is finished. Two adjacent pairs are woven together, the left pair held in the left hand and the right pair in the right. In directions, pairs are numbered left to right. Numbers indicate board position, not actual bobbins. The first row of drawings shows the steps to a half stitch plait. These occur in the sampler in series of six, made by plaiting all the pairs as you did prs 1-2 (prs 3-4, pin at No. 2, prs 5-6, pin at No. 3, and so on).

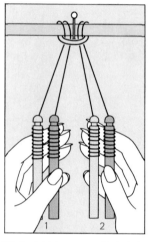

Start weaving, as illustrated above, with pair 1 held in the left hand and pair 2 in the right; pin the other bobbins out of the way.

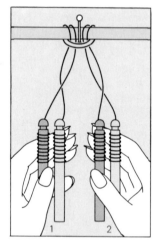

Begin the **half stitch** (written t,c) with a *twist*, worked as follows: push right member of each pair over left with thumb of each hand.

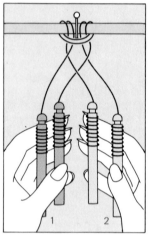

In the *cross*, inside members exchange places, the one on the left crossing over the one on the right. This completes one half stitch.

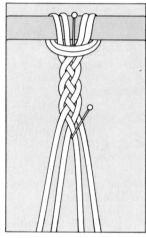

To produce a plait, make half stitches as described down the pricking to the first hole. Place a pin at No. 1 between the two pairs.

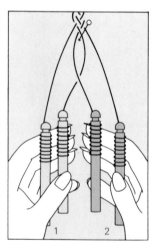

In whole (or cloth) stitch (written c,t,c), pairs are crossed, twisted, then crossed again. The illustration above shows the first *cross*.

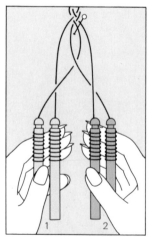

All crosses and twists are worked exactly the same for whole stitch as for half stitch. The *twist* is being worked in the drawing above.

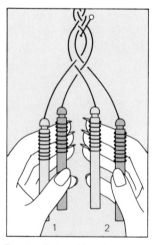

The step illustrated here is the second *cross*, which completes the whole stitch. A plait cannot be made with a whole stitch. When it

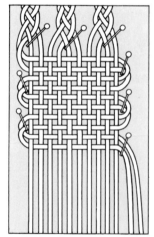

is repeated, the result is **whole stitch ground**, (fourth stitch area in sampler). For whole stitch ground instructions, see p. 72.

Weaving a design

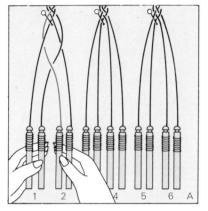

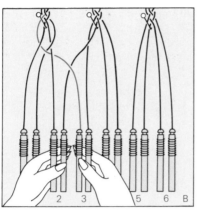

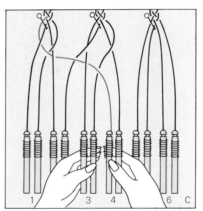

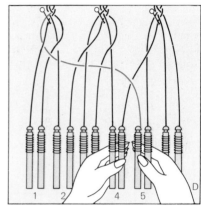

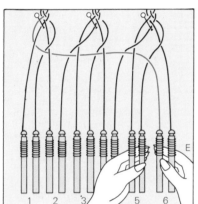

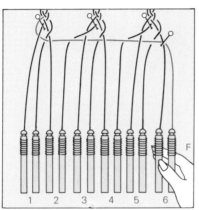

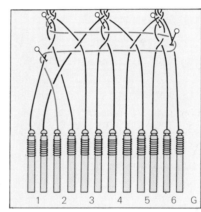

This sequence, of basic steps to half stitch ground, is designed to give a general sense of the interaction of pairs of bobbins. The drawings also clarify what is meant by numbers signifying positions of bobbins on board, not actual bobbins. Space limitations permit showing only 6 pairs of bobbins instead of the 12 used in the sampler, but the principles are the same. In A, the half stitch (t,c) has been completed with prs 1-2; B, C, D and E show half stitches made with prs 2-3, 3-4, 4-5 and 5-6 respectively; in illustration F, the left-to-right sequence has been pinned. (Unless otherwise indicated, pins are always placed between the two pairs of bobbins involved in the just-completed stitch.) In illustration G, half stitches have been worked in reverse (prs 6-5, 5-4, 4-3, 3-2, 2-1). Stitch is worked the same way regardless of direction. This sequence, repeated, produces the ground.

Pinning within a design

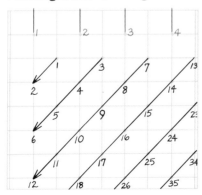

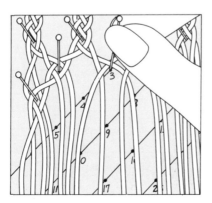

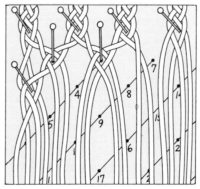

Another pinning principle is demonstrated by torchon ground, a mesh form of the whole stitch ground. It is worked diagonally, making it necessary to place a pin in the centre of each whole stitch to hold it in place. The mesh is created by twisting both pairs of bobbins before each whole stitch; the twists force the stitches apart, producing diamond-shaped holes. Edge bobbins are also given an extra twist for added firmness. The drawings show only the start of the procedure; for full instructions, see next page. To begin the stitch, t,c prs 3-2, pin at No. 1, t,c. This makes a whole stitch with a pin at its centre, both pairs having been twisted first. Then t,c prs 2-1, pin at No. 2, t,c, extra twist to pr 1 (the edge pair). t,c prs 5-4, pin at No. 3, t,c, and so on down the second diagonal row.

Bobbin lace techniques

Ground patterns

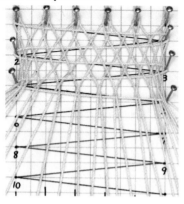

Half stitch ground

Plaits are worked at start and between sections. See p. 69 for positions, p. 70 for technique.

Half stitch ground (also net or lattice ground).
1. t,c prs 1-2 (lay down pr 1, shift pr 2 to left hand and take up pr 3 in right); t,c prs 2-3 (shift prs again); t,c prs 3-4, 4-5, etc., to prs 11-12; pin at No. 1 between 11-12. Twist pr 12 once more (extra twist makes edge firmer); pull slightly on all bobbins to make threads lie even. *Remember numbers signify board position, not actual bobbins.*
2. Work back across row the same way: t,c prs 12-11, 11-10, 10-9, 9-8, etc., to prs 2-1. Pin at No. 2 between prs 2 and 1, extra twist to pr 1.
3. Repeat these two rows until space is filled, ending with pin No. 11.

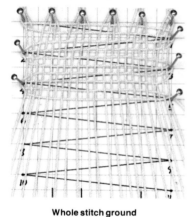

Whole stitch ground

Whole stitch ground (also cloth stitch) worked over an area looks like a woven fabric. In this stitch (written c,t,c), pairs are crossed, then twisted, then crossed again.
1. c,t,c prs 1-2, 2-3, 3-4, etc., to prs 11-12. Pin at No. 1 between prs 11-12, twist pr 12 once more.
2. Work back across row the same way: c,t,c prs 12-11, 11-10, 10-9, etc., to prs 2-1. Pin at No. 2, extra twist to pr 1.
3. Repeat rows 1 and 2 to pin No. 11. Occasionally pull down on threads to keep tension even. *In this stitch, an 'active' pair passes back and forth through the other 'passive' pairs. Variations can be achieved by twisting active, or passive, or both, between stitches or groups of stitches.*

Square hole ground (or whole stitch and twist), a variation of the whole stitch ground, is worked exactly as above, except both pairs of bobbins are twisted once before each whole stitch is made. The twists force the whole stitches apart, making 'square holes'.
1. t,c,t,c prs 1-2, 2-3, 3-4, etc., to prs 11-12. Put a pin between prs 11-12 at No. 1. Edge bobbins do not get extra twists in this pattern.
2. Work back across row the same way: t,c,t,c prs 12-11, 11-10, 10-9, etc., to prs 2-1. Put a pin between prs 2-1 at No. 2.
3. Repeat rows 1 and 2 to pin No. 11. Pull threads into position carefully after every row. Do this by pulling down on the bobbins, not by pulling the threads themselves.

Square hole ground

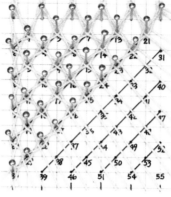

Torchon ground

Torchon ground is like square hole ground, except worked diagonally, making it necessary to put a pin in the centre of each w st to hold it in place.
1. t,c prs 3-2, pin at No. 1, t,c (makes a w st with a pin in its centre, both prs having been twisted first); t,c prs 2-1, pin at No. 2, t,c. Extra twist to pr 1.
2. t,c prs 5-4, pin at No. 3, t,c; t,c prs 4-3, pin at No. 4, t,c; t,c prs 3-2, pin at No. 5, t,c; t,c prs 2-1, pin at No. 6, t,c. Extra twist to pr 1.
3. t,c prs 7-6, pin at No. 7, t,c; t,c prs 6-5, pin at No. 8, t,c; t,c prs 5-4, pin at No. 9, t,c; t,c prs 4-3, pin at No. 10, t,c; t,c prs 3-2, pin at No. 11, t,c; t,c prs 2-1, pin at No. 12, t,c. Extra twist to pr 1.
4. Continue, always picking up the two prs of bobbins on either side of 1st hole for each new diagonal row. Remember to give pr 12 an extra twist before making stitch at No. 31, etc., so each edge has 2 twists.

Brussels ground sequence is the same as for torchon ground, except Brussels ground has two whole stitches at each pin, with pin placed between them.
1. t,c,t,c prs 3-2, pin at No. 1, t,c,t,c (extra twist made after the pin because you cannot cross the same prs twice without twisting them first); t,c,t,c prs 2-1, pin at No. 2, t,c,t,c. No extra twist needed to prs 1 and 12 in this pattern.
2. t,c,t,c prs 5-4, pin at No. 3, t,c,t,c; t,c,t,c prs 4-3, pin at No. 4, t,c,t,c; t,c,t,c prs 3-2, pin at No. 5, t,c,t,c; t,c,t,c prs 2-1, pin at No. 6, t,c,t,c.
3. Continue in this way, always starting each new diagonal row by picking up the prs of bobbins on either side of 1st hole.

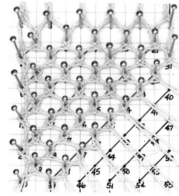

Brussels ground

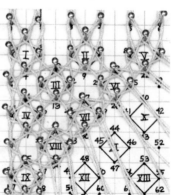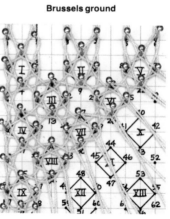

Virgin ground

Virgin ground (or Rose ground) is worked in a series of large diamonds, each in a 'box'. Whole stitches with a twist between are worked in each corner of diamond and pinned in centre. Corners of boxes are completed with one half stitch (no pins).
1. t,c prs 2-3, pin at No. 1, t,c; extra twist pr 1, t,c prs 1-2, pin at No. 2, t,c; t,c prs 3-4, pin at No. 3, t,c; t,c prs 2-3, pin at No. 4, t,c; Diamond I complete. Extra twist pr 1, t,c prs 1-2, pin at No. 5, t,c; t,c prs 3-4. Lower corners of box around Diamond I are now complete. Begin Diamond II.
2. t,c prs 6-7, pin at No. 6, t,c; t,c prs 5-6, pin at No. 7, t,c; t,c prs 7-8, pin at No. 8, t,c; t,c prs 6-7, pin at No. 9, t,c; t,c prs 7-8 and prs 5-6 to complete lower corners of box around Diamond II.
3. t,c prs 4-5, pin at No. 10, t,c; t,c prs 3-4, pin at No. 11, t,c; t,c prs 5-6, pin at No. 12, t,c; t,c prs 4-5, pin at No. 13, t,c; t,c prs 3-4 and prs 5-6.
4. t,c prs 2-3, pin at No. 14, t,c; extra twist pr 1, t,c prs 1-2, pin at No. 15, t,c; t,c prs 3-4, pin at No. 16, t,c; t,c prs 2-3, pin at No. 17, t,c; extra twist pr 1, t,c prs 1-2, pin at No. 18, t,c; t,c prs 3-4.
5. Continue same way with Diamond V, giving pr 12 an extra twist for a firmer edge. Each diamond begins with prs on either side of its 1st (top) hole – prs 10 and 11 for Diamond V. As Diamond IX, XII, XIII are completed, put pins under half stitches at holes No. 57-62 to hold them in place for next section.

Other lace techniques

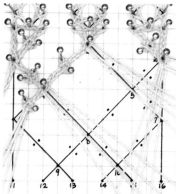

Plaited lace

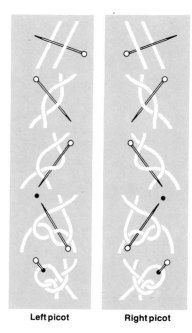

Left picot   **Right picot**

Windmill join

Plaited lace is simply half stitch plaits enhanced with tiny picots and joined. Begin by making a plait with prs 1-2 long enough to reach pin No. 1. Do not put in a pin yet, but lay the plait aside, and make a plait with prs 3-4 halfway to pin No. 1. The two holes at this point mark the positions for the picots.

Left and right picots are made with the left and right pairs of bobbins – see diagram. Use a pin to help pull up the loop as shown; then insert pin in the loop and pull down carefully on the two bobbins to lock the picot in place. Continue making the plait to pin No. 1 and then join this plait to the first by means of a 'windmill join' (below).

The windmill join is just a whole stitch, with a pin in its centre, made with each pair of bobbins functioning as a single bobbin. Cross pr 2 over pr 3; cross pr 4 over pr 3 and pr 2 over pr 1 (this is the twist). Put pin in No. 1. Cross pr 2 over pr 3. Join is now completed. Repeat this procedure with prs 9 to 12, putting another join at No. 2. With prs 5 to 8, make plaits and join at No. 3. Continue making plaits, picots and joins where indicated on the pricking. At pins No. 11 to No. 16, place pins between the pairs of bobbins in each plait to hold them in position for the next section.

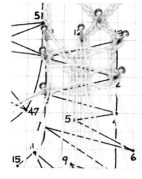

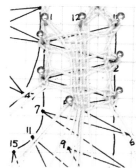

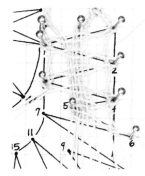

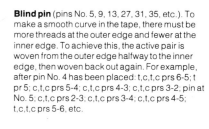

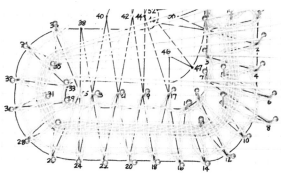

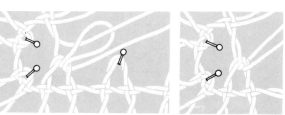

Braid or tape lace, a style popular in Russia and Eastern Europe, is characterised by curving lines and free forms. Although apparently complex, designs require only a few pairs of bobbins, just enough for the width of the tape, which turns, curves and joins to itself by means of 'sewings' (below). The tape is made like whole stitch ground, varied by twisting the pairs to make openings. Before starting, remove all centre pins from the ground patterns, and push the pins right in along both edges. Cover the completed lace, but leave the pricking exposed where you will be working the tape. You will be making two sections, one at each side, with six pairs of bobbins for each; 6th pair is active for left side, 1st pair for right. Pin the right-side bobbins out of the way – left side is made first. When thread runs out on active weavers, turn into passive, then join a new thread and work old and new together for a few rows. Cut off old ends.

Making the tape:
1. t,c,t,c prs 6-5, t pr 5; c,t,c prs 5-4, 4-3, 3-2; t,c,t,c prs 2-1; pin at No. 1.
2. t,c,t,c prs 1-2, t pr 2; c,t,c prs 2-3, 3-4, 4-5; t,c,t,c prs 5-6; pin at No. 2.

Blind pin (pins No. 5, 9, 13, 27, 31, 35, etc.). To make a smooth curve in the tape, there must be more threads at the outer edge and fewer at the inner edge. To achieve this, the active pair is woven from the outer edge halfway to the inner edge, then woven back out again. For example, after pin No. 4 has been placed: t,c,t,c prs 6-5; t pr 5; c,t,c prs 5-4; c,t,c prs 4-3; c,t,c prs 3-2; pin at No. 5; c,t,c prs 2-3; c,t,c prs 3-4; c,t,c prs 4-5; t,c,t,c prs 5-6, etc.

Sewings. As the tape curves, it must be joined to itself at intervals with 'sewings', made by joining the active pair of bobbins to previously made portion of tape at a pin. Sewings are made here at pins No. 6, 8, 17, 19, 21, 23, 25, etc. These pins are placed further than usual from the edge of the tape, and best given one or two extra twists for added firmness. Pins No. 6 and 8 are joined on the other side, so the first sewing comes after pin No. 36. When it has been placed, weave through tape as usual towards pin No. 25; extra twist to active pr. Remove pin at No. 25; with crochet hook, reach down through loop at No. 25 and pull up thread of nearest bobbin. Insert other bobbin through pulled-up thread, then gently pull both threads back in position. Replace pin at No. 25, and continue weaving as usual. Sewings are sometimes made without an extra twist on the pair: e.g., at No. 49, where a sewing is made to No. 1; at No. 51, where one is made into the plait; along edges of ground patterns, where tape is joined to sampler edges. After completing tape, finish off dowel by making a plait with each group of 4 bobbins long enough to go around it. End with sewing made through base of plait with each pair acting as a single bobbin. Tie prs in tight reef knot; clip close.

Lace
weaves

Introduction
Materials
Setting up the loom
Preparing the weft
The weaves

Introduction

Lace can be created by the technique of weaving, which is the interlacing of two sets of threads, the warp and the weft, to produce a textile. In most forms of weaving, all warp threads are parallel to each other and all weft threads are parallel to each other, with the warp and the weft at right-angles to one another. In lace weaving, warp and weft are diverted somewhat from their parallel course to form spaces in the weave. The resulting textile is an openwork form of lace.

Lace weaving can be worked on a simple frame loom or a complex mechanical one. Whichever loom is used, lace weaving is manoeuvred by the weaver. The technique, in fact, is called weaver-controlled or finger-controlled because, to manipulate warp or weft threads, the weaver uses her fingers or a stick-like instrument rather than the mechanism of the loom.

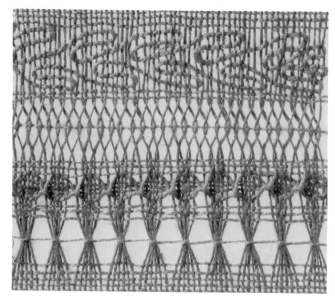

The woven lace sampler, left, incorporates a variety of the lace weaves shown on pp. 76–77. They are, from top to bottom: Spanish lace, Mexican lace, Danish medallion and Brook's bouquet.

Materials

Lace weaves can be worked on any loom. The purpose of the loom is to keep the warp threads evenly spaced and under tension while the weft is passed over and under them. We chose to work on a frame loom because it is simple to use and inexpensive. The weaves shown on pp. 76–77, however, can be woven on almost any loom you may have.

To make a frame loom, you will need canvas stretcher bars, available at art shops in different sizes. You will need one set of two bars for the width of the frame, and one set of two bars for the length of the frame. To decide what size frame you need for the size weaving you want to make, see p. 75. To assemble the stretcher bars into a frame loom, see p. 75.

For the weaving process, you will also need a shuttle, a tool used for carrying the weft; a shed sword or shed stick, a tool used to help in manipulating the warp threads; and appropriate thread.

Canvas stretchers, sold at artists' suppliers, can be used to make a frame loom.

A shuttle is a flat wooden stick with a deep indentation at each end; the weft thread is wrapped on the shuttle (see p. 75)

Yarns for lace weaving include fine, strong linen thread in sizes 10/1, 10/2 or 10/5.

A shed sword or pick-up stick is a flat stick pointed at one end. It is slightly longer than width of weaving.

Lace weaves

Setting up the loom

On a frame loom, the maximum size of the textile you can weave is slightly less than the dimensions of *the frame opening*. Maximum width is 2 to 5 cm less; maximum length is about 15 cm less because warp threads become too tight to work with as a consequence of what is called *take up*. Take up is the small amount of warp that is used up as the warp threads curve over and under the weft. Since stretcher bars, which are 4 cm wide, are sold by their outside length measurement, you must use a frame that is larger than the size weaving you want. If, for example, you want to weave a 25 by 40 cm textile, you will need a 40 by 65 cm stretcher frame.

To estimate the amount of warp thread needed, multiply warp threads per centimetre (see Step 2, below) by width of weaving by *length of loom*. To estimate the amount of weft, multiply weft threads per centimetre by width of weaving by *length of weaving*.

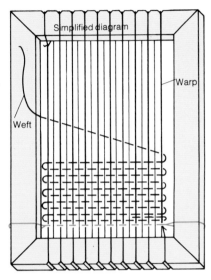

Weaving is the interlacing of weft threads and warp threads. On a frame loom, warp threads are first wrapped around the loom so they are held taut. Weft is woven over and under the warp.

Preparing the weft

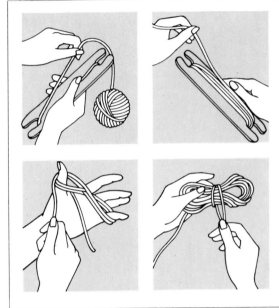

To wind thread on to a shuttle, hold thread end against shuttle with your thumb (left). Wind thread around shuttle so thread end is secured (right). Continue winding thread, making sure you do not pull it as you wind. Do not wind too much thread on shuttle or it will not pass easily through the warp.

To make a butterfly, wind thread in a figure-eight around your thumb and little finger (left). Slip the bundle off your fingers and secure it in the centre with a rubber band (right).

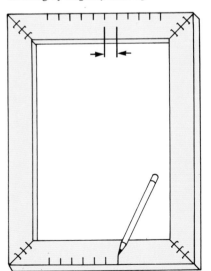

1. Assemble the stretcher bars by fitting the corners together. Be sure corners make a true square; staple them to secure the joins. With a pencil, mark off centimetres along top and bottom of the frame on the outer edge.

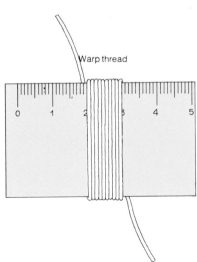

2. To determine number of warp threads per centimetre, wind thread around ruler. Count wraps; multiply by width to be woven. Divide amount in half to give numbers of threads for front and back of loom.

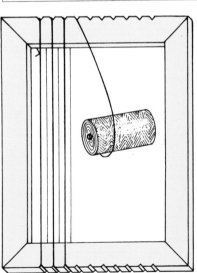

3. Mark threads per centimetre along frame top. With small saw, make a notch at each mark; sand frame. Tie warp to frame at top left. Bring warp down the front, around bottom edge, and up the back, keeping thread in the notches.

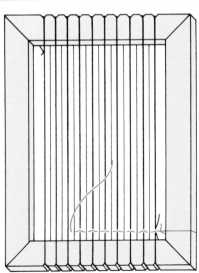

4. As you warp the loom, keep the tension slack but not loose. Threads are now in two layers – in front of and behind loom. To make them one layer, weave a piece of string, called a heading, over top and under bottom threads. Tie at sides.

The weaves

Plain weave is the simplest weave; the weft goes over one warp thread and under the next across the row. On a frame loom, one shed or space between warp threads is already created by the loom. The first weft shot (term for passage of weft) goes in this shed; pass the shuttle through this space (A), leaving an 8 cm tail. Pack the weft in with a fork. For the next row, weft goes in the *countershed*, created by weaving shed stick *over* threads on top of loom and *under* threads behind it. Turn stick on its side and pass the shuttle through the space made by it (B). Put tail in this shed. Repeat these rows.

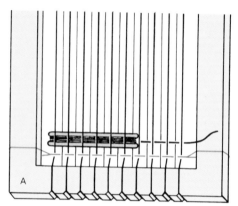

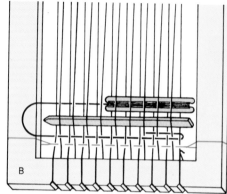

A

B

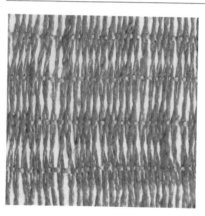

Gauze or leno weave is created by manipulating warp threads so they change places with one another. If *one* warp thread changes places with one other, the lace is 1/1 gauze; if *pairs* of threads change places, the lace is called 2/2. Starting at the right side, pick up the far right thread and bring it to the left over the second thread. Pick up the second thread with the shed stick, letting the first thread fall beneath it. Work across the row in this way (A). Turn stick on its side and insert the weft. Then work a row of plain weave left to right (B). Continue alternating these two rows.

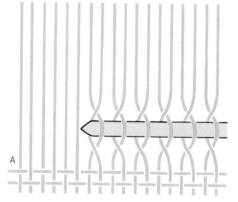

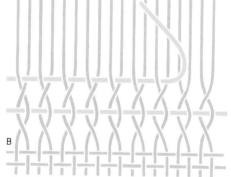

A

B

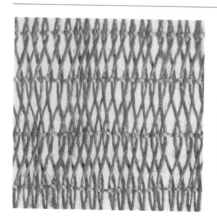

Mexican lace is a variation of the gauze weave. Starting at the right, twist first thread over third, pick up third. To begin pattern, twist second thread over fifth, pick up fifth. Twist fourth thread over seventh, pick up seventh. Continue across the row in this way, twisting the next untwisted even-numbered thread with the next odd-numbered one three threads away (A). Turn the shed stick on its side and insert the weft. Then work a row of plain weave to maintain the twists (B). Repeat these two rows.

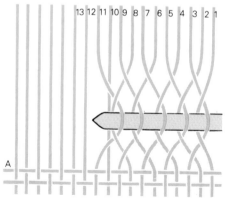

13 12 11 10 9 8 7 6 5 4 3 2 1

13

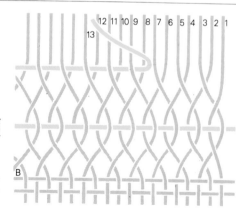

12 11 10 9 8 7 6 5 4 3 2 1

A

B

Lace weaves

The weaves

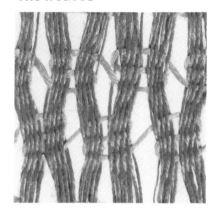

Spanish lace is worked with a butterfly rather than a shuttle. Starting on the right, weave a small group of warp threads in plain weave, going back and forth as many times as you like. Here, it is three times (A). Carry the weft to the next group of warp threads and weave this group the same number of times as the first. Continue across the row this way. Many variations in this pattern can be made with the second row of weaving (B) by changing the groups of threads, varying the number of warp threads in each group, and alternating and splitting groups.

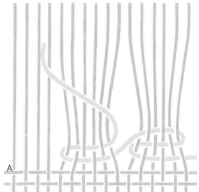

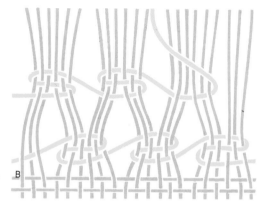

Brook's bouquet is a lace pattern that uses the same technique as backstitch in embroidery. The weft is carried over warp threads and then back under them. Begin this weave after several rows of plain weave. Bring the weft under a group of warp threads, up over the threads, and back under them. Pull the weft to gather the warp threads (A). Continue gathering groups, leaving one warp thread between them as shown here, or no threads between groups. For second row, alternate the placing of groups, centring them between two groups in the previous row (B).

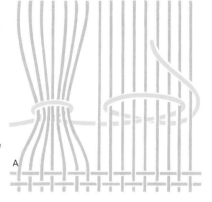

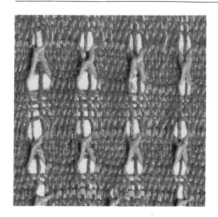

Danish medallion consists mostly of plain weave using two different weft threads. Primary weft thread is usually the same as the warp; secondary weft contrasts in colour, weight or texture. To begin, weave a row of secondary weft from left to right. Change to primary weft and weave several rows of plain weave. Determine where you want the medallions to be; use a crochet hook to pull up a loop of secondary weft half as high as the plain weave (A). Weave secondary weft from right to first loop; pull weft through loop with crochet hook (B). Weave to next loop and pull weft through it. Repeat.

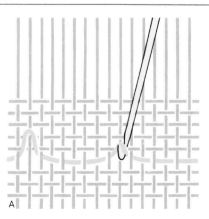

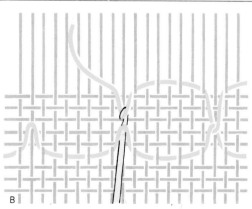

Hairpin crochet lace

Making strips
Joining strips
Finishing edges
Variations

Making strips

Hairpin crochet lace is a type of crochet worked with a two-pronged fork, or hairpin, and a crochet hook. Yarn is wound round the prongs of the hairpin to form a series of large loops held together by a row of crochet stitches worked in the centre, called the spine. The strips produced by this process are then joined together. (See opposite page for methods of joining.) The width of the strips is determined by the distance between the prongs. The hairpins are U-shaped, and available in a wide range of sizes from 10 mm to 100 mm. They may or may not incorporate detachable clips for use at the end of the prongs. (See diagrams below for placing.) The lacy strips can be made from any type of yarn from thin cotton to thick knitting yarn. Directions for the basic crochet stitches are on pp. 9–11.

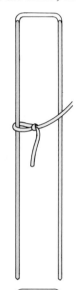

1. To begin, hold the hairpin in the left hand with prongs pointing downwards. Use the metal clip if it is provided with the hairpin. Make a slip knot in the yarn and slide the loop that it forms on to the left prong. Adjust the knot so that it is in the centre between the prongs.

Metal clip

2. Wind the yarn around the right prong, front to back, and hold it taut with your left hand. Insert the crochet hook under the front strand of the loop. Pick up the yarn at the back and bring it through the loop to form a loop on the hook.

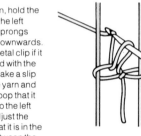

3. With the crochet hook, pick up the yarn at the back again. This is called yarn round hook.

4. Draw the yarn through the loop on the hook; you will have one loop on the hook. This completes the joining of the first loop on the right of the hairpin.

5. Remove the hook from the loop. From the back, insert the hook in the dropped loop. Turn the hairpin from right to left in front of you.

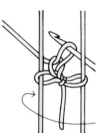

6. Turning the hairpin causes the yarn to wrap round what is now the right prong to form another loop. The crochet hook is now at the front of the hairpin.

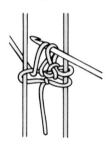

7. This new loop is secured in the centre with a double crochet stitch. To do this; insert hook under front strand of left loop, yarn round hook and draw through the left loop so you have two loops on the hook.

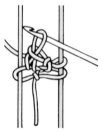

8. Yarn round hook and draw through both loops on the hook. Continue making the strip by repeating steps 5, 6, 7 and 8. Each new loop is formed by turning the hairpin at the completion of double crochet stitch in the centre.

9. When hairpin is full, slide all but the top four loops on both sides off the prongs. Continue working as before.

Attach clip at the end of the prongs.

Remove clip before sliding loops off prongs, then replace.

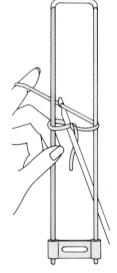

Metal clip

Joining strips

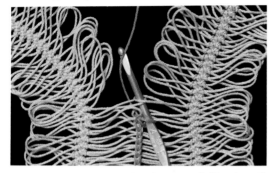

Slipstitch. With a crochet hook and extra yarn held underneath the work, join the strips by inserting the hook into one loop from left and one loop from right strip. Slipstitch them together by catching yarn on hook and drawing it through the three loops.

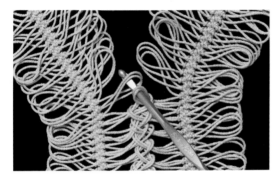

Weaving. This method requires no extra yarn. Insert the crochet hook into one, two or three loops of one strip, then into the same number of loops of the other strip. Draw the second group through the first. Continue along the length of the strips.

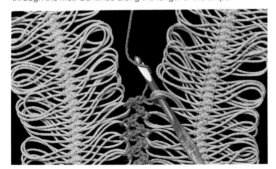

Chain stitch. With a crochet hook and extra yarn, pick up two loops from one strip and work a double crochet stitch (p. 10) in the space. Work 2 chain (p. 9), pick up two loops from the other strip and work a double crochet in the space, 2 chain. Repeat.

Finishing edges

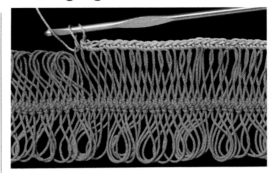

A double crochet stitch along the edge is the simplest way to finish the outside loops of a strip. To do this, make a loop on the hook with a separate length of yarn. Work a double crochet stitch into each loop along the length of the strip.

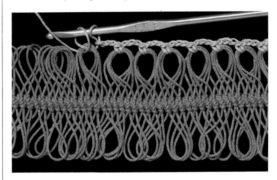

To group the loops, pick up several loops, keeping the twist in them. Work a double crochet stitch in the centre space of the groups of loops. Make a chain between groups of loops that has one stitch less than the number of loops you picked up.

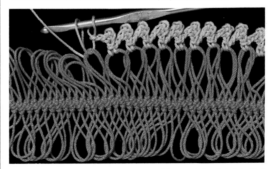

To make a picot edging, work a double crochet stitch into first two loops held together. 4 chain, work a double crochet stitch into third chain from hook, 2 chain, work a double crochet stitch into next two loops held together. Repeat from the 4 chain.

Variations

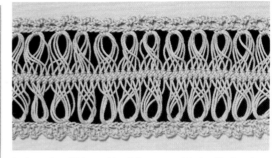

An insertion. Make a strip of the appropriate length. To edge each side, work 1 dc (for abbreviations, see p. 14) in first 4 loops, keeping the twist in them, 3 ch. Repeat for the length of the strip. For second row, work 1 dc in dc of previous row, 3 ch, 1 dc in centre stitch of 3 ch loop, 3 ch. Repeat across row.

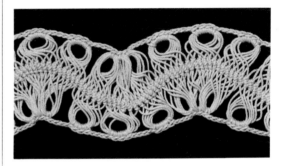

A wavy band. Make a strip of the appropriate length. To edge one side, work (4 dc in 6 loops held together, 4 ch) 3 times, then work (1 dc in 6 loops held together) 3 times, 4 ch. On the other side, start with second group of stitches – double crochet without chain stitches – so groups are opposite each other.

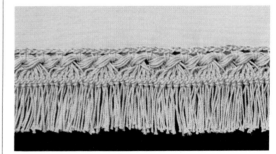

Fringe. Make two strips of the appropriate length. Join the two strips by weaving them together. Fold the resulting band in half so that the weaving is on top. To finish this edge, work 1 dc in the first space, 2 ch, work 1 dc in the next space, 2 ch. Repeat along the strip. For fringe, cut loops along other side of strip.

Index

Back stitch, 46
Bobbin lace, 68–73
  ground patterns, 72
  pinning within a design, 71
  preparing the pricking, 69
  tools and materials, 68
  weaving a design, 71
  winding bobbin pairs, 70

Chain stitch, 8–9
Crochet, 4–48
  assembling and finishing, 46–7
  basics, 6–13
  buttonholes, 45
  buttons, 44
  charting, 38
  edgings and insertions, 47
  geometric shapes, 16–17
  joining sections, 46
  ribbing, 44
  shaping, 15, 42–3
  shorthand symbols, 38
  terminology, 14
Crochet stitches, 18–37
  clusters, 22
  filet crochet, 28
  Irish crochet, 30–1
  Jacquard, 36–7
  loops, 34–5
  meshes, 26–7, 29
  motifs, 23–5
  multicolour, 36–7
  shells, 20–1
  textures, 18–19
  Tunisian crochet, 32–3
Crocheted shapes, 16–17
Crocheting a garment, 39–45
  charting, 40–1
  designing, 39

Double chain stitch, 13
Double crochet, 10
Double-faced treble crochet, 13
Double treble crochet, 11

Filet lace netting, 62–7
  basic techniques, 63–4
  cushion cover, 67
  materials, 62
  plain square mesh, 65
  sampler, 65
  stitches, 66

Hairpin crochet lace, 78–9
Half treble crochet, 10
Hook, 7–9

Irish crochet, 30–1

Jacquard crochet techniques, 36–7

Lace weaves, 74–7
  materials, 74
  preparation, 75
  weaves, 76–7
Left-handed crochet techniques, 9

Multicolour crochet, 36–7

Needlepoint lace, 50–6
  bars and picots, 54
  edgings, 56
  insertions, 55–6
  materials, 50
  meshes, 52–3
  sampler, 51
  stitches, 52–6

Raised crochet stitches, 12

Slipstitch, 11
Stitch, selecting, 18

Tatting, 57–61
  forming double stitch, 58
  materials, 57
  one shuttle, 59–60
  terms and abbreviations, 57
  working with two threads, 61

Tension, testing crochet, 14
Tools and materials
  bobbin lace, 68–7
  crochet, 6–7
  filet lace netting, 62
  lace weaves, 74
  needlepoint lace, 50
  tatting, 57
Treble crochet, 10
Triple treble crochet, 11
Tunisian crochet, 32–3
  blanket, 48

Yarns, 6